WE'RE NOT HERE FOR A LONG TIME ...

WE'RE HERE FOR A GOOD TIME!

First published in 1999 by
Mercier Press
PO Box 5, 5 French Church Street Cork
email: books@mercier.ie
16 Hume Street Dublin 2
email: books@marino.ie
Trade enquiries to CMD Distribution
55A Spruce Avenue
Stillorgan Industrial Park
Blackrock County Dublin
email: cmd@columba.ie

© 'Jimmy' 1999

ISBN 1 85635 289 7

10 9 8 7 6 5 4 3 2 1

A CIP record for this title is available
from the British Library

Cover illustration and design by
Caroline Hyland
Printed by Cox&Wyman, Cardiff Road,
Reading Berks

WE'RE NOT HERE FOR A LONG TIME . . .

WE'RE HERE FOR A GOOD TIME!

JIMMY

MERCIER PRESS

FOREWORD

Well, here it is. My second collection of jokes, funny stories, one-liners and lists from around the world, as brought to you on *The 2FM Breakfast Show*, with Gareth O'Callaghan. I really hope you enjoy it.

To those of you 'Jimmy' fans who have my first collection, *Jimmy's Joke Book*, I think you are in for no surprises, just a lot more laughs. This 'asked for' collection (by my accountant, Bill) contains that same streak of good humour that helps us all see the funny side of life. It's getting close to 5,000 calls now and I must say, the response to my little spot, just after eight o'clock, on Ireland's most-listened-to breakfast show has always delighted me but has never surprised me. The wife Violet says she can't see what all the fuss is about. She's been laughing at my little spot for years! Twelve years, in fact. Hard to believe, but that's how long I've been on the air as 'Mr Ten Past Eight'.

Over the years, but in particular more recently, I have been asked to 'come out of the closet' so to speak and let the listeners have a *look* at Jimmy. I don't think so! Almost every Irish TV show has asked me to appear as a guest, and I'm always being asked by promoters to do one-man shows. I've also been approached by a TV production company to do a cartoon series based on my antics and am frequently asked by newspapers for that 'exclusive' photograph. So far, I've turned them all down. I am, after all, as you know, a very shy person! And we are, after all, talking about radio here and the pure magic of it. So, it's a life on the airwaves for me, I think, and long may it last.

I'll never get that villa in Spain just by cleaning windows!

Jimmy

ACKNOWLEDGEMENTS

My thanks to:

The *2FM Breakfast Show* team: Gareth, for being there, with your *great* sense of humour and *brilliant* broadcasting skills. Go on outta that and Yoooooo-Hooo!

My special thanks to John (Victor) Clarke, Head of 2FM. Thanks, John, for your inspiration, talent, understanding and friendship.

My thanks, of course, to Maggie Stapleton, our very dedicated producer and to Deirdre Magee, who has now phoned *me* more times (in more places!) than she has phoned her husband Noel! Thanks Deirdre, and 'hello' to the boys, Robert and Gavin! My thanks also to broadcasting assistants Trudy Treacy, Carol McGrane, Helen Howard and Jane Reid who from time to time work on the programme ... and I mean that in the nicest possible way girls. And of course, *all* the *excellent* 2FM people, both on-air and off-air talent, whom I've worked with over the years. The Best!

To Gerry Ryan; someone who understands the *power* of radio more than anyone I know ... for support, encouragement and appreciation and of course, all Gerry's wonderful team whom I've worked with on many occasions. A great crew.

My appreciation also to RTÉ's director of radio, Helen Shaw, for vision and support (and for her parking space when she's away on business). Thanks Helen.

My grateful thanks to Jo O'Donoghue, Rachel Sirr and all at Marino Books.

This book would not have been possible without the many contributions from all you loyal 'Jimmy' fans in the Ten Past Eight Gang. Your support and loyalty over the past twelve years means an awful lot to me. My heartfelt thanks.

Finally, to all my family and personal friends who have helped over the years; remember, this is only the beginning and we have a long way to go. But don't worry, I have some great plans, and it's all going to happen.

And of course, to 'Buster' and 'The Princess'. Two people who always put a smile on *my* face. I love you both *so* much.

I always will.

Peace, happiness and love.

Jimmy

TIME

Imagine there is a bank that credits your account each morning with £86,400.

It carries over no balance from day to day.

Every evening it deletes whatever part of the balance you failed to use during the day.

What would you do? Draw out every penny, of course!

Each of us has such a bank. Its name is TIME.

Every morning, it credits you with 86,400 seconds.

Every night it writes off, as lost, whatever of this you have failed to invest to good purpose.

It carries over no balance.

It allows no overdraft. Each day it opens a new account for you.

Each night, it burns the remains of the day.

If you fail to use the day's deposits, the loss is yours.

There is no going back. There is no drawing against the 'tomorrow.'

You must live in the present on *today*'s deposits. Invest it, so as to get from it the utmost in health, happiness, and success!

The clock is running. Make the most of today.

To realise the value of ONE YEAR, ask a student who failed a grade.

To realise the value of ONE MONTH, ask a mother who gave birth to a premature baby.

To realise the value of ONE WEEK, ask the editor of a weekly newspaper.

To realise the value of ONE HOUR, ask the lovers who

are waiting to meet.

To realise the value of ONE MINUTE, ask a person who just missed the train.

To realise the value of ONE SECOND, ask a person who just avoided an accident.

To realise the value of ONE MILLISECOND, ask a person who won a silver medal in the Olympics.

Treasure *every* moment that you have!

And treasure it *more*, because you *shared* it with someone special, special enough to spend your time.

And remember, that time waits for no one.

Yesterday is history,

Tomorrow is a mystery,

Today is a gift, that's why it's called the *present*!

(Unknown)

We're not here for a long time . . . we're here for a good time!

Jimmy

'None of us knows where we're going . . .
but the clever ones have a great time
getting there'

In memory of Dad

Saint Peter was manning the Pearly Gates, when about forty people from the northside of Dublin showed up.

Never having seen anyone from the northside of Dublin at Heaven's door before, Saint Peter asked them all to hold on for a few minutes, because he'd have to check with God.

He bounces off across the clouds to tell God.

After hearing the news, God instructed Peter to admit the ten most virtuous from the group.

'Fair enough,' said Pete, and off he went.

A few minutes later he returns, gasping for breath.

'They're gone, God, they're gone.'

'What? You mean all of the northsiders are gone?' asked God.

'No!' said Saint Peter. The bloody Pearly Gates are gone.'

A man walks into a building and gets into a lift. He presses the button for the fifth floor. At the fifth floor, the most stunning woman he has ever seen gets into the lift and leans seductively against the wall.

The man doesn't know where to look and starts to get very nervous.

The woman begins to unbutton her blouse and throws it on the floor. At this stage, the guy is getting really nervous.

'Make a woman out of me,' she demands, in a most seductive voice.

With that, he unbuttons his shirt, throws it on the floor and says,

'Right, *iron that.*'

A man was eating fish and chips in the street one day when a woman walked past with a small dog.

The dog started yapping at the smell of the man's food.

'Do you mind if I throw him a bit?' asked the man.

'Not at all,' said the lady.

So the man picked the dog up and threw him over a wall!

A 75-year-old man went to see his doctor to get a sperm count. The doctor gave the man a jar and said, 'Take this home and bring me back a sample tomorrow.'

The next day, the 75-year-old man turns up at the doctor's office and gives him the jar, which is as clean and empty as on the previous day.

The doctor asks what happened, and the man explains.

'Well doc, it's like this. First I tried with my right hand, but nothing happened. Then I tried with my left hand, and again, nothing happened. Then I asked my wife for help. She tried with her right hand, but nothing. Then her left, still nothing. She even tried with her mouth, first with her teeth in, then with the teeth out and still nothing. Would you believe, we even asked the lady next door, and she tried with both hands and her mouth too, but still, nothing.'

The doctor was shocked. 'You asked your NEIGH-BOUR?!!'

The old man said, 'Yup, but no matter what we tried, we couldn't get the bloomin' jar open!'

A man was walking down the street one day, when up ahead he noticed a little boy wearing a red fireman's hat, a fireman's badge and sitting in a red trolley, all done up like a fire engine.

It looked like it was being pulled along very slowly, by a large Labrador retriever.

When the man got closer to the lad, he noticed that he had a rope tied around the dog's testicles, which probably accounted for why the dog was walking so gingerly.

Smiling, he spoke to the boy, 'That's a really nice fire engine you have there, son, but I'll bet you that he'd pull you along a lot faster if you tied that rope around his neck instead of his testicles.'

'Oh, I know he would,' said the little boy, 'but then I wouldn't have a siren.'

A man takes his Rottweiler to the vet...

'My dog is very cross-eyed, is there anything you can do for him?'

'Well,' says the vet, 'Let's have a look at him.'

So he picks the dog up and has a good look at its eyes.

'Well,' says the vet, 'I'm going to have to put him down.'

'What? Because he's cross-eyed?'

'No, because he's very bloody heavy.'

A zebra walks into a farm one day, and comes across a pig.

'Hello, I'm Mister Zebra. Who are you and what do you do?' asks the zebra.

'Oh, I just snort and snort and roll in the mud all day,' said the pig.

'Fair enough,' said the zebra. 'Goodbye.'

The zebra then comes across a chicken and says, 'Hi, I'm Mister Zebra . . . who are you?'

'I'm Mister Chicken.'

'And what do you do?' asks the zebra.

'Oh, I just peck, peck, peck all day long,' said the chicken.

'Fair enough,' replied the Zebra. 'Goodbye'.

The zebra then comes across the farm stallion and says, 'Hello, I'm Mister Zebra, who are you?' The stallion stands proudly, braces every muscle in his body and says, 'I'm the farm stallion.'

'And what do you do?' asks the zebra.

The stallion flexes his muscles and says, 'Get those pyjamas off you and I'll show you.'

What's the difference between a crane and a giraffe?
A crane has hydraulics!

Why did the blonde keep staring at the carton of orange juice?

Because it said concentrate.

A woman goes into a funeral home to make arrangements for her husband's funeral.

She tells the director that she wants her husband to be buried in a dark blue suit.

He asks, 'Wouldn't it be easier to bury him in the black suit that he's wearing?'

The woman insists that it must be a blue suit, and gives him a blank cheque to buy one.

When she comes back for the wake, she sees her late husband laid out in the coffin in a beautiful blue suit. She is delighted, and tells the funeral director how happy she is. She then asks how much it cost.

'Actually, it didn't cost a penny,' said the director.

'The funniest thing happened. Just after you were gone the other day, another corpse was brought in, wearing a dark blue suit. I noticed that they were about the same size and asked the other widow if she would mind if her husband was buried in a black suit. She said that was fine with her. So . . . I just switched the heads!

A man is relaxing at home reading his paper, when his wife walks up behind him and smacks him on the back of the head with a frying pan. Roaring with pain, he says, 'What was that for?'

She looks him in the eye and says, 'I found a piece of paper in your pocket with Betty Sue written on it.'

'Jesus, love, said the husband, rubbing his head. Remember last week, when I went to that horse race? Betty Sue was the name of the horse I went there to bet on.'

The wife shrugged her shoulders and walked away. Two days later, he's reading his paper when she walks up behind him and gives him an unmerciful smack on the back of the head with the frying pan again.

'What the hell,' said the husband, doubled over with pain,' What the hell was that for?'

The wife said, 'Your horse just called.'

A woman has twins and gives them up for adoption.

One of them goes to Egypt and is named Amahl. The other goes to a family in Spain, and they name him Juan.

Years later, Juan sends a picture of himself to his birth mom.

Upon receiving the picture, she tells her husband that he wishes she also had a picture of the other boy.

Her husband responds, 'But they're identical twins. If you've seen Juan, you've seen Amahl.'

A drunk staggers into a church and sits down in a confession box, and says nothing.

The bewildered priest coughs to attract the man's attention, but still the man says nothing.

The priest then knocks on the wall three times in a final attempt to get the man to speak.

Finally the drunk replies, 'No use knockin' mate . . . there's no paper in this one either.'

A woman is trying to get on a bus, but her skirt is too tight and she can't step on. So she reaches behind her and lowers the zipper a bit and tries again. Still, the skirt is too tight.

She reaches behind her again, and lowers the zipper some more. She still can't step up on to the bus, so she lowers the zipper for a third time.

Suddenly she feels two hands on her backside, trying to push her on to the bus.

She turns around immediately, and with a shocked look on her face says, 'Excuse me, Sir, but I don't know you well enough for you to do that!'

The man says, 'Listen, Missus, I don't know you well enough for you to unzip my fly three times either!'

A couple were out golfing one day, on a very exclusive course.

The course was lined with million-dollar houses. On the second tee the husband said, 'Listen, love, be very careful when you drive the ball, and make sure you don't hit any windows in those houses, or it will cost us a fortune.'

The wife teed up and sends the ball crashing right through the window of the biggest house on the course.

The husband cringed and said, 'I told you to watch out for the houses! We better go up and apologise and see how much this is going to cost us.'

They walked up, knocked on the door, and heard a voice say, 'Come on in.'

They opened the door and saw glass all over the floor and a broken bottle lying on its side in the foyer. A man sitting on the couch said, 'Are you the people who broke my window?'

'Em, em, yeah, sorry about that,' said the husband.

'No, actually, I want to thank you! I'm a genie, and I've been trapped in that bottle for 3,000 years. You've released me! I'm allowed to grant you three wishes. I'll give you each one wish, and I'll keep the last one for myself.'

'That's great, fair enough,' said the husband. 'I want a million dollars a year for the rest of my life.'

'No problem, it's the least I can do. And you, what do you want?' the genie said, looking at the wife.

'I want a big house in the country, and one in every major city in the world,' she said.

'Consider it done,' the genie replied.

'And what's your wish, genie?' asked the husband.

'Well, since I've been trapped in that bottle, I haven't had sex with a woman. My wish is to sleep with your wife.'

The husband looks at the wife and said, 'Well, we did get our wishes granted, and just think of the great life we'll have with all that money and all those houses. If you don't mind, then I don't mind.'

The wife agrees, and the genie takes her upstairs and ravishes her for about two hours.

After it was all over, the genie rolled over, looked at the wife, and said, 'By the way, how old is your husband, anyway?'

'Thirty-two,' she replied.

'And he still believes in genies . . . that's amazing!'

An Irishman has been at the pub all night, drinking. The barman finally says that the bar is closed. So he stands up to leave and falls flat on his face. He figures he'll crawl outside and get some fresh air, and maybe that will sober him up.

Once outside he stands up and falls flat on his face again. So he crawls all the way home, and up the stairs. When he finally reaches the bed he tries once more to stand up. This time he falls right into the bed and is sound asleep.

The next morning he wakes up to find his wife standing over him and shouting, 'So, you've been out drinking again!!'

'How did you know?' he asked.

'The pub just called,' she said. 'You left your wheelchair there again!'

A woman was in bed with her lover, when she heard her husband opening the front door.

'Hurry,' she said, 'stand in the corner.'

She very quickly rubbed baby oil over him and then dusted him with talcum powder.

'Don't move,' she said, 'until I tell you that it's OK. Just pretend to be a statue.'

As the husband enters the room, he says, 'What's this, honey?'

'Oh, it's just a statue. The Wilsons across the road bought one for their bedroom, and I liked it so much, I decided to get one for ours too.'

Nothing else was said, even later that night when they went to bed.

Around three in the morning the husband got out of bed, went down to the kitchen and returned with a glass of milk and a sandwich.

'Here,' he said to the statue, 'have something to eat. I know what its like. I stood in the Wilsons' house for three days and nobody offered me as much as a glass of water.'

Liam received a parrot for his birthday.

The parrot was fully grown with a very bad attitude and an even worse vocabulary.

Every second word out of him was a curse. Liam tried hard to change the bird's attitude and was constantly saying polite words, playing soft music and basically trying his very best to change the parrot's attitude. Nothing worked.

If he yelled at the bird, the bird got worse. If he shook the bird, the bird got ruder and madder.

Finally, in a moment of desperation, Liam put the parrot in the freezer and closed the door.

For a few moments he heard the bird squawking and screaming and kicking. Then all went quiet.

Liam was getting a bit frightened, so he opened the freezer door, and out walks the parrot on to Liam's extended arm and says, 'I am sorry that I might have offended you with my language, my actions and my whole attitude to life in general, and furthermore I whole-heartedly ask your forgiveness. In future, I will endeavour to correct my behaviour.'

Liam was astounded at the bird's sudden change in attitude and was about to ask him what had changed him . . . when the parrot continued, 'May I ask what the chicken did?'

A man goes to see his doctor and complains about a very bad headache.

'Tell me about it,' says the doctor.

'Well, it's like this, doc. It starts at the back of my head, and moves forward, until it affects my eyes, and for a few minutes I can't see.'

The doctor gives the man a thorough examination and analyses his blood.

'Well,' says the doctor, 'the problem is simple, it's your willy. We'll have to cut it off.'

'No bloody way,' replies the man, 'you're not cutting my willy off.'

And he storms out of the surgery.

He heads off to get a second, third and even a fourth opinion, and all the doctors come to the very same conclusion. The willy has to go. Feeling helpless, the man faces up to the facts and goes for the operation, and the willy is cut off.

A few months later he has to go to the tailor to have a new suit made.

After all the measurements are taken, the tailor asks the man. 'By the way, sir, when you wear your trousers, do you usually put your willy to the left side or the right side?'

Being a bit sensitive about having no willy, he gets upset, and asks what the hell does it matter where he puts it.

The tailor says, 'Well, its better to make more space on the side that you put your willy, so it's more comfortable.'

The man is angry, and asks, 'And what happens if I don't?'

The tailor says, 'Well, then you start getting a bad headache. It starts at the back of your head and moves forward to your eyes ... then you can't see at all for a few minutes.'

A small white guy got into an elevator and noticed a huge black guy standing next to him.

The big black guy looked down at him and said, 'Pleased to meet you. Seven foot tall, 350 pounds, twenty-inch willy, three-pound left ball, three pound right ball, Turner Brown.'

The small guy fainted.

The big guy picks him up and tries to bring him around by slapping his face and asking, 'What's wrong, what's wrong?'

Eventually the little guy comes around and he's mumbling.

'Excuse me, but what did you say?' he asks the big black guy.

The big guy looks down on him and says, 'Seven foot tall, 350 pounds, twenty-inch willy, three-pound left ball, three-pound right ball, Turner Brown.'

The little guy sighed, 'Oh sweet *Jesus*, thank God! I thought you said *Turn around*!!'

A man is sitting at home one evening when the doorbell rings. When he answers the door, a six-foot-tall cockroach is standing there.

The cockroach immediately punches him in the face and scampers off.

The next evening the man is sitting at home when the doorbell rings again. When he answers it, the cockroach is there again, and this time it spits at him, punches him and gives him several karate chops before running away.

The third evening, the man is relaxing at home, when the bell rings again. As soon as he opens the door, the cockroach lunges at him and stabs him half a dozen times before making off.

The poor man is in bits but manages to crawl to the telephone and phone an ambulance. He is rushed to intensive care and they manage to save his life. The next morning, the doctor is doing his rounds. He asks the man what happened, so the man explains about the six-foot cockroach's attacks, culminating in the near-fatal stabbing.

The doctor thinks for a moment and says, 'Yes. There's a nasty bug going around at the moment, all right.'

Back in the forties, a farmer and his wife went to a fair. The farmer was fascinated by the aeroplanes and the air show. He just couldn't resist asking a pilot how much it would cost for a ride.

'Ten pound for three minutes,' replied the pilot.

'That's far too much,' said the farmer.

The pilot thought for a second and then said, 'I'll make a deal with you. If you and your wife can manage to keep totally silent for the three minutes, the ride will be free. But if you even make a sound, you'll have to pay the tenner.'

The farmer and his wife agreed, and went for a fantastic flight.

After they landed, the pilot said to the farmer, 'I want to congratulate you for not making a sound. You're a very brave man.'

'Thanks very much,' said the farmer, 'but I have to tell you, I nearly screamed when the wife fell out.'

A man walks into an emergency room with two black eyes and a five iron wrapped tightly around his throat.

Naturally, the doctor asked him what happened.

'Well, it was like this,' said the man.

'I was having a quiet round of golf with my wife when she sliced her ball into a pasture of cows. We went to look for it and while I was rooting around I noticed one of the cows had something white at its rear end. I walked over and lifted up the tail and sure enough, there was my wife's golf ball, stuck right in the middle of the cow's arse. That's when I made my mistake.'

'What did you do?' asked the doctor.

'Well, I lifted the tail and yelled to the missus, "This one here looks like yours!"'

HAVE YOU EVER NOTICED?

Signs of the Times

On a vet's door: Back in five minutes. Stay. Sit.

In a laundromat: Automatic washing machines. Please remove all your clothes when the light goes out.

In a butcher's window: Our tongue sandwiches speak for themselves.

In a taxidermist's window: We really know our stuff.

On a maternity room door: PUSH, PUSH, PUSH.

On an electrician's van: Let us remove your shorts.

In a bowling alley: Please be quiet. We need to hear a pin drop.

Outside a computer shop: Back in five minutes. Gone for a quick byte.

In a health food shop window: Closed due to illness.

In a field: The farmer allows walkers to cross the field for free, but the bull charges.

Outside a second-hand shop: We exchange anything –
Bicycles, Washing machines, etc. Why not bring your wife
along and get a wonderful bargain?

On a fence: Salesmen welcome. Dog food is expensive.

There was this man who was in a horrible accident and was injured.

But the only permanent damage he suffered was the amputation of both of his ears.

As a result of this unusual handicap, he was very self-conscious about his having no ears.

Because of the accident, he received a large sum of money from the insurance company.

It was always his dream to own his own business, so he decided with all this money he had, he now had the means to own a business. So he went out and purchased a small, but expanding computer firm. But, soon afterwards he realised that he had no business knowledge at all, so he decided that he would have to hire someone to run the business.

He picked out three top candidates, and interviewed each of them.

The first interview went really well. He really liked this guy. His last question for this first candidate was, 'Do you notice anything unusual about me?'

The guy said, 'Now that you mention it, you have no ears.'

The man got really upset and threw the guy out.

The second interview went even better than the first. This candidate was much better than the first. Again, to conclude the interview, the man asked the same question, 'Do you notice anything unusual about me?'

This guy also noticed. 'Yes, you have no ears.'

The man was really upset again, and threw this second candidate out.

Then he had the third interview. The third candidate

was even better than the second, the best out of all of them. Almost certain that he wanted to hire this guy, the man once again asked, 'Do you notice anything unusual about me?'

The guy replied, 'Yeah, you're wearing contact lenses'.

Surprised, the man said, 'Wow! That's quite perceptive of you! How could you tell?'

The guy burst out laughing and said, 'Well, you can't wear glasses if you don't have any ears!'

Woman being interviewed at social welfare office:

Q. 'Are you married?'

A. 'No, I'm divorced.'

Q. 'And what did your husband do before you divorced him?'

A. 'A lot of things I didn't know about.'

A married couple went to the hospital together to have their baby delivered.

Upon their arrival, the doctor said he had invented a new machine that would transfer a portion of the mother's pain to the father. He asked if they were willing to try it out. They were both very much in favour of it.

The doctor set the knob to 10 per cent for starters, explaining that even 10 per cent was probably more pain than the father had ever experienced before. But as the labour progressed, the husband felt no pain, so he asked the doctor to go ahead and bump the machine up a notch.

The doctor obliged and adjusted the machine to 20 per cent pain transfer. The husband was still feeling fine. The doctor checked the husband's blood pressure and pulse and was amazed at how well he was doing. At this, they decided to try for 50 per cent.

The husband continued to feel quite well. Since it was obviously helping out his wife considerably, he encouraged the doctor to transfer ALL the pain to him. The wife delivered a healthy baby with virtually no pain. She and her husband were ecstatic.

When they got home, the postman was dead on their doorstep.

A couple of drinking buddies, who are aeroplane mechanics at Dublin Airport, are in the hangar.

Somehow, it gets fogged in and they have nothing to do.

One of the guys says to the other, 'God, I'd love a drink ... have you anything with you?'

'Nah, afraid not,' says the other fella, 'but I hear that you can drink jet fuel, and it'll give you a bit of a buzz'.

So they crack open a container and get stuck in and have a great time.

The following morning, one of them wakes up and he just knows that his head will explode if he gets up. But it doesn't. He gets up and he feels good. In fact, he feels great. No hangover.

The phone rings and it's his buddy. The buddy says, 'Hey, how do you feel?'

'I feel great,' he replies, and the buddy says, 'I feel great too!'

'You don't have a hangover?

'No, that jet fuel is great stuff ... and no hangover ... we ought to do this more often.'

'Yeah, we could,' says the buddy on the phone, 'but there's just one thing ... did you fart yet?'

'No, eh, why?' came the reply.

'Well DON'T, 'cause *I'm* phoning from Galway.'

Paddy Irishman, Paddy Englishman and Paddy Scotsman have just reached the final test in their bid to join the Foreign Legion.

At the test centre, Paddy Englishman is summoned first.

He is brought into a room. Handing a gun to him the examiner says, 'If you go in through that door, you will find your wife; shoot her dead and you're a fully fledged member of the Legion.'

Paddy Englishman replies, 'Dear God, no, she is my wife, the mother of my children, I couldn't possibly do that!'

So the examiner replies, 'Well in that case, I'm afraid you have failed in your bid to join the Foreign Legion.'

Next in is Paddy Scotsman, who is given the same task but replies, 'Och, nooo, my dear wife, how could I?' So Paddy Scotsman also fails the test.

Finally, Paddy Irishman is given the task, and he duly grabs the shotgun, bursts into the room and slams the door behind him.

The examiner then hears two shotgun blasts, and then hears screaming and banging and shouting, followed by a long silence. With that the examiner bursts into the room, and sees Paddy standing over his dead wife. 'What on earth have you done!' screams the examiner.

Paddy Irishman replies, 'Your shotgun was only loaded with blanks, so I had to strangle her to death!!'

Two men meet in the street, and the first fella says, 'The mother-in-law is after getting a nice job down in the dairy.'

'That's terrific,' says the second fella, 'what's she doing?'

'Well,' says the first fella, 'she's working on a milk round, but it's not permanent. It's only until the horse gets better.'

A woman's husband has been slipping in and out of a coma for several months, yet she stayed by his bedside every single day. When he came to, he motioned for her to come nearer.

As she sat by him, he said, 'You know what? You have been with me all through the bad times. When I got fired, you were there to support me. When my business fell, you were there. When I got shot, you were by my side. When we lost the house, you gave me support. When my health started failing, you were still by my side.

'You know, the more I think about it now, I think you bring me terrible bad luck.'

Gaybo, Gerry and Gareth are all down below in hell, for the bad lives they have led.

The devil escorts them through various corridors and eventually stops in a hall with three doors.

At the first door he calls Gareth up, opens the door and inside is this absolute hound of a woman. A witch, old and craggy, with boils, hair in the wrong places, just the ugliest thing you've ever seen. A voice is heard to say, 'Gareth, you have spent a life of ill-repute and debaucherous behaviour. You are damned to spend eternity with this old hag.' Off goes a forlorn-looking Gareth.

At the second door, Gaybo is called forward. The door opens and an even uglier looking woman is inside. Balding with big hairy moles and open sores and no teeth and she's just awful.

A voice is heard, 'Gay, you have spent a life of sin, lust, drink and drugs, you are damned to spend eternity with this old hag.' Off the dejected Gaybo goes.

Lastly, Gerry Ryan walks to the final door and is very, very nervous.

The door opens to reveal the sumptuous Marian Finucane, dressed in stockings and suspenders ... the whole lot.

Gerry immediately livens up and a voice is heard, 'Marian Finucane, you have spent a life of sin ... '

Five blondes walk into a bar. The first one goes up to the barman and asks for five pina coladas.

She brings the drinks down to her friends, they each take a glass and shout, '51 days hooray.'

The second blonde goes up to the bar and orders the same, she also gives one to each friend and again they shout, '51 days hooray.'

The third and fourth blonde go to the bar and do the same.

The barman, now watching them, starts to wonder what's going on, so when the fifth blonde goes to the bar, he asks, 'What's 51 days?'

'Well,' says the blonde 'We bought a jigsaw and it said 2–4 years on the box, but *we* did it in 51 days.'

A man phones his local waste disposal company, and says, 'I want a skip outside my house for the next three days.'

And the voice at the other end says, 'Go ahead, no one's stopping you.'

A man is out in the wilderness of China and he's hopelessly lost.

It's been nearly three weeks since he's eaten anything besides what he could forage, and he's been reduced to sleeping in caves and under trees.

One afternoon he comes upon an old mansion in the woods. It has vines covering most of it and the man can't see any other buildings in the area. However, he sees smoke coming out of the chimney, implying someone is home.

He knocks on the door and an old man answers, with a beard almost down to the ground. The old man squints his eyes and says, 'What do you want?'

The man says, 'I've been lost for the past three weeks and haven't had a decent meal or sleep since that time. It would be most gracious of you if I could have a meal and sleep in your house for tonight.'

The old Chinese man says, 'I'll let you come in on one condition: You cannot mess around with my granddaughter.'

The man, exhausted and hungry, readily agrees, saying, 'I promise I won't cause you any trouble. I'll be on my way first thing in the morning.'

The old Chinese man counters, 'Okay, but if I do catch you then I'll give you the three worst Chinese torture tests ever known to man.'

'Okay, okay,' the man says as he enters the old house. Besides, he thinks to himself, what kind of woman would live out in the wilderness all her life?

Well, that night, when the man comes down to eat (after showering), he sees how beautiful the granddaughter is. She is an absolute pearl, and while he had only been lost three weeks, it had been many, many months without companionship. And the girl had only seen the occasional monk besides her grandfather and well, they both couldn't keep their eyes off each other throughout the meal.

That night, the man snuck into the girl's bedroom and they had quite a time, but kept the noise down to a minimum. The man crept back to his room later that night thinking to himself, Any three torture tests would be worth it after *that* experience.

Well, the next morning the man awoke to a heavy weight on his chest.

He opened his eyes and there was this huge rock on his chest. On the rock was a sign saying, '1st Chinese torture test, 100 lb rock on your chest.'

What a lame torture test, the man thought to himself as he got up and walked over to the window. He opened the shutter and threw the rock out.

On the other side of the rock is another sign saying, '2nd worst Chinese torture test, rock tied to right testicle.'

The man, seeing that the rock was too far out the window to be grabbed, jumps out the window after the rock.

Outside the window is a third sign saying, '3rd worst Chinese torture test, left testicle tied to bedpost!'

A nun gets into a cab in New York.

She demurely says in a small, high voice, 'Could you please take me to Times Square?'

The cabby initiates conversation. 'Hey sista, that's kinda a long drive? You mind if we, like, chat?'

The nun says, 'Why no my son, whatever is on your mind?'

The cabby says, 'About dis celibacy thing. You tellin' me you never think about *doin' it*?'

The nun says, 'Why certainly, my son, the thought has crossed my mind a time or two. I am of weak human flesh you understand.'

The cabby says, 'Well, would'ya ever consider, you know, *doin' it*?'

The nun says, 'Well, I suppose under certain conditions, in a very unique circumstance, I might consider it.'

The cabby says, 'Well, what would those conditions happen to be?'

The nun says, 'Well, he'd have to be Catholic, unmarried and well, certainly, he could have no children.'

The cabby says, 'Well, sista, today is your lucky day. I am all three. Why don't you come on up here ... I won't even make you really break ya vows. All ya gotta do is show me a good time, know what I mean?'

The nun looks around ... they are awfully far away from where anyone would recognise her ... At the next light she gets into the front with the driver.

By the next light, the nun is getting back into the rear of the cab, and the cabby is smiling from ear to ear.

As she settles in, the nun hears the cabby begin to laugh.

The nun enquires, 'Why, my son, what is so humorous?'

The cabby sneers, 'Sista, I got ya. I'm Protestant, married, and I got four kids.'

And from the back of the cab comes the nun's low-voiced response, 'Yeah, well my name is Dave and I'm on my way to a fancy-dress party.'

Howard had felt guilty all day long. No matter how much he tried to forget about it, he couldn't. The guilt and sense of betrayal was overwhelming.

But every once in a while he'd hear that soothing voice trying to reassure him, 'Howard. Don't worry about it. You aren't the first doctor to sleep with one of his patients and you won't be the last.'

But invariably the other voice would bring him back to reality, 'Howard. You're a veterinarian!'

A man walks into a pharmacy and asks for a pack of condoms. As soon as he has paid for them, he starts laughing and walks out.

The next day, the same performance, with the man walking out laughing, fit to burst.

The pharmacist thinks this is odd and asks his assistant, if the man returns, to follow him.

Sure enough, he comes into the store the next day, repeating his actions once more. The assistant duly follows. Half an hour later, he returns.

'So did you follow him?'

'I did.'

'And . . . where did he go?'

'Over to your house . . . '

A man stumbles up to the only other patron in a bar and asks if he could buy him a drink.

'Why of course,' comes the reply.

The first man then asks, 'Where are you from?'

'I'm from Ireland,' replies the second man.

The first man responds, 'You don't say. I'm from Ireland too! Let's have another round to Ireland.'

'Of course,' replies the second man.

Curious, the first man then asks, 'Where in Ireland are you from?'

'Dublin,' comes the reply.

'I can't believe it,' says the first man. 'I'm from Dublin too! Let's have another drink to Dublin.'

'Of course,' replies the second man.

Curiosity again strikes and the first man asks, 'What school did you go to?'

'Saint Mary's,' replies the second man. 'I graduated in 1962.'

'This is unbelievable!' the first man says. 'I went to Saint Mary's and I graduated in '62, too!'

About that time in comes one of the regulars and sits down at the bar.

'What's been going on?' he asks the bartender.

'Nothing much,' replies the bartender. 'The O'Malley twins are drunk again!'

Three blondes were walking through the forest when they came upon a set of tracks.

The first blonde said, 'Diane, those are deer tracks.'

The second blonde said, 'No, Elaine, those are elk tracks.'

The third blonde said, 'You're both wrong, those are moose tracks.'

The blondes were still arguing when the train hit them.

A man was helping one of his cows give birth, when he noticed his four-year-old son standing wide-eyed at the fence, taking in the whole event. The man thought, 'Great ... he's four and I'm going to have to start explaining the birds and bees. No need to jump the gun – I'll just let him ask, and I'll answer.

After everything was over, the man walked over to his son and said, 'Well son, do you have any questions?'

'Just one,' gasped the still wide-eyed lad. 'How fast was that calf going when he hit that cow?'

Late one night, a burglar broke into a house that he thought was empty.

He tiptoed through the living room, but suddenly he froze in his tracks when he heard a loud voice say, 'Jesus is watching you!'

Silence returned to the house, so the burglar crept forward again.

'Jesus is watching you', the voice boomed again.

The burglar stopped dead again. He was frightened. Frantically, he looked all around.

In a dark corner, he spotted a bird cage and in the cage was a parrot.

He asked the parrot, 'Was that you who said Jesus is watching me?'

'Yes,' said the parrot. The burglar breathed a sigh of relief, then he asked the parrot, 'What's your name?'

'Clarence,' said the bird.

'That's a dumb name for a parrot,' sneered the burglar. 'What idiot named you Clarence?'

The parrot said, 'The same idiot who named the Rottweiller Jesus.'

Paddy Englishman, Paddy Irishman and Paddy Scotsman went for a job on a building site.

Paddy Englishman went in first, and the foreman asked him a question.

'If I gave you one rabbit on a Monday and one rabbit on a Tuesday, how many rabbits would you have?'

Paddy Englishman replied, 'Two,' and the foreman said, 'Well done.'

Paddy Scotsman went in next, and the foreman asked him the same question, and he also replied, 'Two.'

Paddy Irishman went in and the foreman asked him, 'If I gave you two rabbits on consecutive days, how many rabbits would you have?'

Paddy Irishman said the question was a bit complicated, so the foreman said, 'If I gave you one rabbit on a Monday and one rabbit on a Tuesday, how many rabbits would you have?'

Paddy Irishman replied, 'Four.' Again, the foreman asked him the same question and again Paddy Irishman replied, 'Four.' The foreman said he really wanted to give him the job and asked him again.

'If I gave you one rabbit on Monday and one rabbit on Tuesday, how many rabbits would you have? So Paddy Irishman again replied, 'Four.'

The foreman asked how the hell could he have four rabbits if he gave him one on a Monday and one on a Tuesday and Paddy Irishman replied, 'Sure, I have two already!'

The Pope met with his cardinals to discuss a proposal from Benjamin Netanyahu, the leader of Israel.

'Your Holiness,' said one of the cardinals, 'Mr Netanyahu wants to challenge you to a game of golf to show the friendship and ecumenical spirit shared by the Jewish and Catholic faiths.'

The Pope thought it was a good idea, but he had never held a golf club in his hand. 'Have we not,' he asked, 'a cardinal who can represent me against the leader of Israel?'

'None that plays golf very well,' a cardinal said. 'But,' he added, 'there *is* a man named Jack Nicklaus, an American golfer who is a devout Catholic. We can offer to make him a cardinal, then ask him to play Benjamin Netanyahu as your personal representative. In addition to showing our spirit of cooperation, we'll also win the match.'

Everyone agreed it was a good idea. The call was made. Of course, Nicklaus was honoured and agreed to play. The day after the match, Nicklaus reported to the Vatican to inform the Pope of the result.

'I have some good news and some bad news, Your Holiness,' said the golfer.

'Tell me the good news first, Cardinal Nicklaus,' said the Pope.

'Well,' Your Holiness, 'I don't like to brag, but even though I've played some pretty terrific rounds of golf in my life, this was the best I have ever played, by far. I must have been inspired from above. My drives were long and true, my irons were accurate and purposeful and my putting was perfect. With all due respect, my play was truly miraculous.'

'The bad news?' the Pope asked.

Nicklaus sighed. 'I lost to Rabbi Tiger Woods, by three strokes.'

An eighty-year-old man was having his annual check-up and the doctor asked him how he was feeling.

'I've never been better!' he boasted. 'I've got an eighteen-year-old bride who is pregnant and having my child! What do you think about that?'

The doctor considered this for a moment, then said, 'Let me tell you a story. I knew a guy who was an avid hunter. He never missed a season. But one day he went out in a bit of a hurry and he accidentally grabbed his umbrella instead of his gun.'

The doctor continued, 'So he was in the woods and suddenly a grizzly bear appeared in front of him! He raised up his umbrella, pointed it at the bear and squeezed the handle. And do you know what happened?' the doctor queried.

Dumbfounded, the old man replied, 'No.'

The doctor continued, 'The bear dropped dead in front of him!'

'That's impossible!' exclaimed the old man. 'Someone else must have shot that bear.'

'That's kind of what I'm getting at ... ' replied the doctor.

48

A Jack Russell terrier goes into the dole office and hops up onto the counter and to the amazement of the clerk asks if he can sign on for the dole.

The clerk asks the Jack Russell to hang on for a minute and goes and rings a friend of his in the circus. He tells his mate that it's incredible but he has a talking Jack Russell at the counter wanting to sign on; his circus friend tells him to ask the dog to come over straight away.

The clerk goes back to the Jack Russell and tells him that he has a bit of good news as he has managed to get him a job in the circus.

The Jack Russell is quite surprised and says to the clerk, 'What does a plasterer want a job in the circus for?'

A man is at work one day when he notices that his male co-worker is wearing an earring.

This man knows his co-worker to be a normally conservative fellow, and is curious about his sudden change in fashion sense.

'Yo, Bob, I didn't know you were into earrings.'

'Oh, yeah, sure,' says Bob sheepishly.

'Really? How long have you been wearing one?'

'Ever since my wife found it in our bed.'

A fellow tries to cross the Mexican border on a bicycle with two big bags balanced on his shoulders. The guard asks, 'What's in the bags?'

The fellow says, 'Sand!'

The guard wants to examine them. The fellow gets off the bike, places the bags on the ground, opens them up, and the guard inspects them … only to find sand.

The fellow packs the sand, places the bags on his shoulders, and pedals the bike across the border.

Two weeks later, the same scenario is repeated …

'What have you there?'

'Sand.'

'We want to examine.'

Same results … nothing but sand and the fellow is on his way again.

Every two weeks for six months the inspections continue.

Finally, one week the fellow doesn't show up. However, the guard sees him downtown, in a bar, and says to the fellow, 'Buddy, you had us crazy. We sort of knew you were smuggling something. I won't say anything if you tell me. I just need to know … what were you smuggling?'

The fellow says, 'Bicycles.'

A Scottish guy named Frank finds himself in dire trouble. His business has gone bust and he's in serious financial trouble. He's so desperate that he decides to ask God for help. He begins to pray . . .

'God, please help me. I've lost my business and if I don't get some money, I'm going to lose my house as well. Please let me win the Lotto.'

Lotto night comes and somebody else wins it.

Frank again prays . . .

'God, please let me win the Lotto! I've lost my business, my house and I'm going to lose my car as well'.

Lotto night comes and Frank still has no luck.

Once again, he prays . . .

'My God, why have you forsaken me? I've lost my business, my house, and my car. My wife and children are starving. I don't often ask you for help and I have always been a good servant to you. PLEASE just let me win the Lotto this one time so I can get my life back in order.'

Suddenly there is a blinding flash of light as the heavens open and Frank is confronted by the voice of God Himself: 'Frank, at least meet me *halfway* on this. Buy a ticket.'

A wealthy playboy met a beautiful young girl in an exclusive lounge. He took her to his lavish apartment where he soon discovered she was not a tramp, but was well groomed and apparently very intelligent. Hoping to get her into bed, he began showing her his collection of expensive paintings and first editions by famous authors and offered her a glass of wine.

He asked whether she preferred port or sherry and she said, 'Oh, sherry by all means.'

'To me it's the nectar of the gods. Just looking at it in

a crystal-clear decanter fills me with a glorious sense of anticipation. When the stopper is removed and the gorgeous liquid is poured into my glass, I inhale the enchanting aroma and I'm lifted on the wings of ecstasy.

It seems as though I'm about to drink a magic potion and my whole being begins to glow.

'The sound of a thousand violins being softly played fills my ears and I'm transported into another world . . . On the other hand, port makes me fart.'

Esmerelda arrives home with the shopping and pulls out a wok from her bag.

'Are you cooking Chinese tonight?' Quasimodo asks excitedly.

'Don't be silly!' Esmerelda replies. 'It's to help me iron your shirts!'

A man goes to his doctor and tells him that his wife hasn't wanted to have sex with him for the last seven months.

The doc tells the man to bring his wife in so he can talk to her. So the wife comes into the doctor's office and the doctor asks her what's wrong, and why doesn't she want to have sex with her husband anymore.

The wife tells him, 'For the last seven months every morning I take a taxi to work. I don't have any money so the taxi driver asks me, 'So are you going to pay today or what?' So I take a 'or what.' When I get to work I'm late so the boss asks me, 'So are we going to write this down in the book or what?' So I take a 'or what.' Going home, I take the taxi and again I don't have any money so the taxi driver asks me again, 'So are you going to pay this time or what?' So I again take a 'or what.' So you see doc, when I get home I'm all tired out, and I don't want it any more.'

The doctor thinks for a second and then turns to the wife and says, 'So, are we going to tell your husband about this . . . or what?'

A kid comes home from school with a writing assignment.

He asks his father for help. 'Dad, can you tell me the difference between *potential* and *reality*?'

His father looks up, thoughtfully, and then says, 'I'll display it to you. Go and ask your mother if she would sleep with Robert Redford for a million dollars. Then go ask your sister if she would sleep with Brad Pitt for a million dollars. Then come back and tell me what you've learned.'

The kid is puzzled, but he decides to see if he can figure out what his father means.

He asks his mother, 'Ma, if someone gave you a million dollars, would you sleep with Robert Redford?'

His mother looks around slyly, and then with a little smile on her face says, 'Don't tell your father but yes, I would.'

Then he goes to his sister's room and asks her, 'Sis, if someone gave you a million pounds, would you sleep with Brad Pitt?'

His sister looks up and says, 'Omigod! Definitely!'

The kid goes back to his father and says, 'Dad, I think I've figured it out. *Potentially*, we're sitting on two million quid, but in *reality*, we're living with two floozies.'

Two men are talking one day, and one can't decide what to get his wife for her birthday.

She already *has* everything, and besides, she can afford to buy anything she wants, so I'm really stumped,' said the anxious husband.

'I have an idea,' said his friend. 'Why not make up a certificate yourself that says that she can have two hours of great sex, any way and anywhere she wants it. She'll be delighted!'

So his friend did just that.

Next day they meet. 'Well, how did you get on with my suggestion?'

'Oh, she *loved* it,' said the husband. 'In fact she jumped up, wrapped her arms around me, kissed me on the mouth, and ran out the door shouting, "See you in a couple of hours!"'

A pretty young lady was having a tooth pulled. The dentist gave her the usual 'This won't hurt a bit' routine before bending over her with a hand.

He immediately drew back in complete alarm.

'Miss,' he said in a barely audible whisper, 'You have hold of my testicles!'

'Yes, doc, I know,' she smiled, 'and we aren't going to hurt each other, are we?'

Recently, I took some friends out to dinner to a popular restaurant.

Shortly after we were seated, I couldn't help but notice that all the waiters and waitresses, wine-waiters and bellboys were carrying a spoon in their top pocket.

Being very curious, I called our waiter and asked, 'Why the spoons?'

'Well,' he explained, 'our parent company recently hired some consulting efficiency experts to review all our procedures, and after months of statistical analyses, they concluded that our customers drop spoons on the floor 82 per cent more often than any other utensil, at a frequency of four spoons per hour per workstation. By preparing all our workers for this contingency in advance, we can cut our trips to the kitchen down and save time . . . nearly 1.5 extra man-hours per shift.'

Just as he concluded, a 'ch-ching' came from the table behind him, and he quickly replaced a fallen spoon with the one from his pocket. 'I'll grab another spoon the next time I'm in the kitchen, instead of making a special trip,' he proudly explained.

I was impressed. 'Thanks, I hope you don't mind, but I just had to ask.'

'No problem,' he answered, then he continued to take our orders.

As the members of my dinner party took their turns, my eyes darted back and forth from each person ordering, and my menu. That's when, out of the corner of my eye, I spotted a thin, black thread protruding from our waiter's fly.

Again, I dismissed it, yet I had to scan the room and,

sure enough, there were other waiters and wine-waiters with strings hanging out of their trousers.

My curiosity overrode discretion at this point, so before he could leave I had to ask.

'Excuse me, but ... eh ... why, or what ... about ... eh ... you know yourself ... ?'

'Oh, yeah,' he began in a quieter tone. 'Not many people are that observant. That same efficiency group found we could save time in the men's room, too.'

'How's that?' I asked.

'You see', replied the waiter, 'by tying a string to the end of our, eh, selves, we can pull it out at the urinals literally hands-free and thereby eliminate the need to wash our hands, cutting time spent in the restroom by over 85 per cent!'

'Oh, that makes sense,' I said, but then thinking through the process, I asked, 'Hey, wait a minute. If the string helps you pull it out, how do you get it back in?'

'Well,' he whispered, 'I don't know about the other guys, but I use my spoon.'

A businesswoman explained her delicate problem to the doctor.

She was always breaking wind at board meetings, during interviews, in lifts and on trains and buses. It was impossible to control.

'But at least I am fortunate, in two respects,' she told the doctor. 'They neither smell nor make a noise. In fact, since I have been in your office talking to you, it has happened twice, doctor.'

The doctor reached for his notebook, scribbled a prescription and handed it to her.

She read it. 'What? Nasal drops?' she queried.

'Yes,' said the doc. 'We'll fix your nose first and then have a go at your hearing.'

A three-legged dog walks into a saloon in the Old West. He sidles up to the bar and announces, 'I'm looking for the man who shot my paw.'

A mangy-looking guy goes into a bar and orders a drink.

The barman says, 'No way. I don't think you can pay for it.'

The guy says, 'You're right. I don't have any money, but if I show you something you haven't seen before, will you give me a drink?'

The barman says, 'Only if what you show me is not too risqué.'

'Deal!' says the guy and reaches into his coat pocket and pulls out a hamster.

He puts the hamster on the bar and it runs to the end of the bar, down the bar, across the room, up the piano; then it jumps on the keyboard and starts playing Gershwin songs. And the hamster is really good.

The barman says, 'You're right. I've never seen anything like that before. That hamster is really brilliant on the piano.'

The guy downs the drink and asks the barman for another.

'Money or another miracle, or else no drink,' says the barman. The guy reaches into his coat again and pulls out a frog. He puts the frog on the bar, and the frog starts to sing. He has a marvellous voice and great pitch. A fine singer. A stranger from the other end of the bar runs over to the guy and offers him £300 for the frog.

The guy says, 'It's a deal.' He takes the money and gives the stranger the frog.

The stranger runs out of the bar, delighted with himself. The barman says to the guy, 'Are you some kind of nut? You sold a singing frog for £300? It must have been worth millions. You must be crazy.'

'Not really,' says the guy. 'The hamster is also a ventriloquist.'

A depressed young woman was so desperate that she decided to end her life by throwing herself into the sea.

When she went down to the docks, a handsome young sailor noticed her tears and took pity on her. He said, 'Look, you've got a lot to live for. I'm off to America in the morning, and if you like, I can stow you away on my ship. I'll take good care of you and bring you food every day.'

Moving closer, he slipped his arm around her shoulder and added, 'I'll keep you happy, and you'll keep me happy.' The girl sniffed and nodded yes.

After all, what did she have to lose? That night, the sailor brought her aboard and hid her in a lifeboat. From then on, every night he brought her some sandwiches and pieces of fruit and they made passionate love until dawn. Three weeks later, during a routine search, she was discovered by the captain.

'What are you doing here?' the captain asked.

'I have an arrangement with one of your sailors,' she explained. 'He's taking me to America, and in return I'm letting him screw me.'

'You certainly are,' replied the captain. 'This is the Aran Islands ferry!'

Stevie Wonder and Jack Nicklaus are in a bar. Nicklaus turns to Wonder and says, 'How is the singing career going?'

Stevie Wonder says, 'Not too bad, the latest album has gone into the Top 10 so all in all I think it is pretty good. By the way, how's the golf?'

Nicklaus replies, 'Not too bad. I am not winning as much as I used to but I am still making a bit of money. I have had some problems with my swing but I think I have got that right now.'

Stevie Wonder says, 'I always find that when my swing goes wrong I need to stop playing for a while and not think about it, then the next time I play it seems to be alright.'

Jack Nicklaus says, 'You play golf!'

Stevie Wonder says, 'Yeah, I have been playing for years.'

And Nicklaus says, 'But I thought you were blind, how can you play golf if you are blind?'

Wonder replies, 'I get my caddy to stand in the middle of the fairway and he calls to me. I listen for the sound of his voice and play the ball towards him, then when I get to where the ball lands, the caddy moves to the green or further down the fairway and again I play the ball towards his voice.'

'But how do you putt,' says Nicklaus.

'Well,' says Stevie, 'I get my caddy to lean down in front of the hole and call to me with his head on the ground and I just play the ball towards his voice.'

Nicklaus says, 'What is your handicap.'

Stevie says, 'Well, I play off scratch.'

Nicklaus is incredulous and he says to Stevie, 'We must play a game some time.'

Wonder replies, 'Well people don't take me seriously so I only ever play for money, and actually I never play for less than $100,000 a hole.'

Nicklaus thinks about it and says, 'OK. I'm game for that, when would you like to play?'

Stevie turns around and says, 'I don't mind, any night next week suits me.'

A man placed some flowers on the grave of his dearly departed mother and started back towards his car when his attention was diverted to another man kneeling at a grave.

The man seemed to be praying with profound intensity and kept repeating, 'Why did you have to die? Why did you have to die?'

The first man approached him and said, 'Sir, I don't wish to interfere with your private grief, but this demonstration of pain is more than I've ever seen before. For whom do you mourn so deeply? A child? A parent?'

The mourner took a moment to collect himself, then replied ...

'My wife's first husband.'

A scouser was touring America on holiday and stopped in a remote bar in the hills of Nevada.

He was chatting to the bartender when he spied an old Indian sitting in the corner. He had tribal gear on, long white plaits and had a wrinkled face.

'Who's your man?' asked the scouser.

'That's the Memory Man,' said the bartender. He knows everything. He can remember any fact. Go on, try him out.'

So the scouser goes over, thinking he won't know about English football.

'Who won the 1965 FA Cup Final?' he asks.

'Liverpool,' replies the Memory Man.

'Who did they beat?'

'Leeds,' was the reply.

'And the score?'

'2-1.'

'Who scored the winning goal?'

'Ian St John,' was the old man's reply.

The scouser was knocked out by this and told everyone back home about the Memory Man when he got back.

A few years later he went back to America and tried to find the impressive Memory Man. Eventually he found the bar, and sitting in the same seat was the old Indian, only this time he was older and more wrinkled. Because he was so impressed the scouser decided to greet the Indian in his native tongue. He approached him with the greeting, 'How.'

The Memory Man replied, 'Diving header in the six-yard box.'

A beautiful young woman went into the hospital for a minor operation.

On the day of her operation, the nurses prepared her and wheeled her down to the operating theatre, and left her lying outside on a trolley for a few minutes.

While she was lying there, a young man in a white coat came along, lifted her gown up and began to examine her naked body. He then went away and consulted with another colleague in a white coat. They both returned and examined her again. A third colleague was called over, and he too began to examine her.

By this time, the young lady was becoming quite frustrated at the long wait for her operation and inquired from the white-coated individuals, 'Look, I don't mind you examining me, but when is this bloody operation going to start?'

'We haven't got a clue, luv, came the reply, we're just the painters.'

A priest wanted to raise money for his church and being told that there was fortune in horse racing, he decided to purchase a horse and enter him in the race.

However, at the local auction, the going prices for horses were so steep that the priest ended up buying a donkey.

He figured that since he had bought it, he might as well go ahead and enter it in the races.

The donkey came in third.

The next day, the daily racing form carried this headline:

PRIEST'S ASS SHOWS

The priest was so pleased with his donkey that he entered it in the race again.

This time he won. The daily racing form headlines read:

PRIEST'S ASS OUT IN FRONT

The bishop was so upset with this kind of publicity that he ordered the priest not to enter the donkey in another race. That day's racing form headlines read:

BISHOP SCRATCHES PRIEST'S ASS

This was too much for the bishop and he ordered the priest to get rid of the animal. So the priest decided to give it to a nearby convent.

The next day's racing form headlines read:

NUN HAS BEST ASS IN TOWN

The bishop fainted. He informed the nun that she would have to dispose of the donkey. She finally found a farmer who was willing to buy the animal for £10. The next day, the racing form headlines read:

NUN PEDDLES ASS FOR A TENNER

The bishop passed away and they buried him. The next day, the racing form headlines read:

TOO MUCH ASS RESPONSIBLE FOR BISHOP'S DEATH

A linguistics professor was lecturing to his class one day.

'In English,' he said, 'a double negative forms a positive. In some languages, though, such as Russian, a double negative is still a negative. However, there is no language wherein a double positive can form a negative.'

A voice from the back of the room piped up, 'Yeah, right.'

Phyl, who was a rather well-proportioned secretary, spent almost all of her holiday sunbathing on the roof of her hotel. She wore a bathing suit the first day, but on the second, she decided that no one could see her way up there, and she slipped out of it for an overall tan. She had hardly begun when she heard someone running up the stairs. She was lying on her stomach, so she just pulled a towel over her rear.

'Excuse me, miss,' said the flustered assistant manager of the hotel, out of breath from running up the stairs. 'The Hilton doesn't mind you sunbathing on the roof, but we would very much appreciate your wearing a bathing suit as you did yesterday.'

'What difference does it make?' Phyl asked rather calmly. 'No one can see me up here, and besides, I'm covered with a towel.'

'Not exactly,' said the embarrassed man. 'You're lying on the dining-room skylight.'

A ninety-year-old man is sitting on a park bench, sobbing, when a young man walks by and asks him what's wrong. Through his tears the old man answers, 'I'm in love with a twenty-five-year-old woman.'

'What's wrong with that?' asks the young man.

Between his sobs and sniffles, he answers. 'You don't understand. Every morning before she goes to work, we make love ... At lunchtime she comes home and we make love again, and then she makes my favourite meal. In the afternoon when she gets a break, she rushes home and we make love again, the best an old man could want. And then at suppertime, and all night long, we make love.'

He breaks down, no longer able to speak.

The young man puts his arm around him. 'I don't understand. It sounds like you have the perfect relationship. Why are you crying?'

The senile old man answers, again through his tears, 'I can't remember where I live.'

Sam has been in the computer business for twenty-five years and is finally sick of the stress.

He quits his job and buys fifty acres of land in Vermont as far away from humanity as possible.

Sam sees the postman once a week and gets groceries once a month.

Otherwise, it's total peace and quiet.

After six months or so of almost total isolation, he's finishing dinner when someone knocks on his door. He opens it and there is a big, bearded Vermonter standing there.

'Name's Enoch ... Your neighbour from four miles over the ridge ... Having a party Saturday ... thought you'd like to come.'

'Great,' says Sam, 'after six months of this I'm ready to meet some local folks. Thank you.'

As Enoch is leaving he stops. 'Gotta warn you there's gonna be some drinkin!' he says.

'Not a problem ... after twenty-five years in the computer business, I can do that with the best of them.'

Again, as he starts to leave Enoch stops. 'More 'n likely gonna be some fightin', too.'

Damn, Sam thinks ... tough crowd. 'Well, I get along with people, I'll be there. Thanks again.'

Once again Enoch turns from the door. 'I've seen some wild sex at these parties, too.'

'Now *that's* not a problem,' says Sam, 'Remember I've been alone for six months! I'll definitely be there ... by the way, what should I wear to the party?'

Enoch stops in the door again and says, 'Whatever you want, it's just gonna be the two of us!'

The phone rings at KGB headquarters . . .

'Hello?'

'Hello, is this KGB?'

'Yes. What do you want?'

'I'm calling to report my neighbour Yankel Rabinovitz as an enemy of the state. He is hiding undeclared diamonds in his firewood.'

'This will be noted,' replies a gruff voice.

Next day, the KGB goons come over to Rabinovitz's house. They search the shed where the firewood is kept, break every piece of wood, find no diamonds, swear at Yankel Rabinovitz and leave.

The phone rings at Rabinovitz's house.

'Hello, Yankel! Did the KGB come?'

'Yes.'

'Did they chop your firewood?'

'Yes, they did.'

'Okay, now its your turn to call. I need my vegetable patch ploughed.'

Before going to Europe on business, a man drove his Rolls Royce to a downtown New York City bank and went in to ask for an immediate loan of $5,000.

The loan officer, taken aback, requested collateral and so the man said, 'Well then, here are the keys to my Rolls Royce.'

The loan officer promptly had the car driven into the bank's underground parking for safe keeping, and gave him $5,000.

Two weeks later, the man walked through the bank's doors, and asked to settle up his loan and get his car back.

'That will be $5,000 in principal, and $15.40 in interest,' the loan officer said. The man wrote out a check and started to walk away.

'Wait, sir,' the loan officer said, 'while you were gone, I found out you are a millionaire. Why in the world would you need to borrow $5,000?'

The man smiled. 'Where else could I park my Rolls-Royce in Manhattan for two weeks and pay only $15.40?'

There was an old married couple who had lived happily together for nearly forty years.

The only friction in their marriage was caused by the husband's habit of breaking wind nearly every morning as he awoke. The noise would always wake up his wife and the smell would cause her eyes to water as she would choke and gasp for air. Nearly every morning he told her that he couldn't help it.

She begged him to see a doctor to find out if anything could be done but the husband wouldn't hear of it. He told her that it was just a natural bodily function and then he would laugh in her face as she tried to wave the fumes away with her hands.

She told him that there was nothing natural about it and if he didn't stop, he would fart out his guts one day. Each day, she told him the same thing.

The years went by and the wife continued to suffer and the husband continued to ignore her warnings about farting his guts out, until one Thanksgiving morning, before dawn, the wife went downstairs to prepare the family feast. She fixed pumpkin pie, mashed potatoes, gravy and of course, the turkey.

While she was taking out the turkey's innards, a thought occurred to the wife as to how she might solve her husband's problem.

With a devilish grin on her face, she placed the turkey guts into a bowl and quietly walked upstairs hours before her husband would awake. While he was still soundly asleep, she pulled back the covers and then gently pulled back her husband's jockey shorts. She then placed all the turkey guts into her husband's underwear, pulled them up and replaced the covers and tiptoed downstairs to finish preparing the family meal.

Several hours later she heard her husband awake with his normal loud butt-trumpeting.

This was soon followed by a blood-curdling scream and the sound of frantic footsteps as her husband ran to the bathroom. The wife could not control herself and her eyes began to tear up as she rolled on the floor laughing. After years of putting up with him she had finally gotten even.

About twenty minutes later, her husband came downstairs in his blood-stained underpants with a look of horror in his eyes. She bit her lip to keep from laughing and she asked him what was the matter.

He said, 'Honey, you were right . . . all those years you warned me and I didn't listen to you.'

'What do you mean?' asked his wife.

'Well, you always did tell me that I would end up farting my guts out one of these days and today it finally happened. But with God's help and these two fingers, I think I got 'em all back in!'

Why do married men gain weight and bachelors don't?

Bachelors go to the refrigerator, see nothing they want, then go to bed.

Married guys go to bed, and see nothing they want, then go to the refrigerator.

Becky was on her deathbed, with her husband Jake at her side.

He held her cold hand and tears silently streamed down his face. Her pale lips moved.

'Jake,' she said.

'Hush,' he quickly interrupted, 'don't talk.' But she insisted.

'Jake,' she said in her tired voice. 'I have to talk. I must confess.'

'There is nothing to confess,' said the weeping Jake. 'It's all right. Everything's all right.'

'No, no. I must die in peace. I must confess, Jake, that I have been unfaithful to you.'

Jake stroked her hand. 'Now, Becky, don't be concerned. I know all about it,' he sobbed. 'Sure why else would I poison you?'

A woman was terribly overweight, so her doctor put her on a diet.

'I want you to eat regularly for two days, then skip a day, and repeat this procedure for two weeks. The next time I see you, you'll have lost at least five pounds.'

When the woman returned, she shocked the doctor by losing nearly thirty pounds.

'Why, that's amazing!' the doctor said. 'Did you follow my instructions?'

The woman nodded. 'I'll tell you though, I thought I was going to drop dead that third day.'

'From hunger, you mean?'

'No, from skipping.'

A group of third, fourth and fifth graders accompanied by two female teachers went on a field trip to the local racetrack to learn about thoroughbred horses and the supporting industry.

During the tour some of the children wanted to go to the toilet so it was decided that the girls would go with one teacher and the boys would go with the other.

As the teacher assigned to the boys waited outside the men's toilet, one of the boys came out and told her he couldn't reach the urinal. Having no choice, she went inside and began hoisting the little boys up by their armpits, one by one.

As she lifted one, she couldn't help but notice that he was unusually well-endowed for an elementary school child. 'I guess you must be in the fifth,' she said.

'No ma'am,' he replied, 'I'm in the seventh, riding Silver Arrow, but thanks for the lift up anyway.'

Once upon a time, a beautiful, independent, self-assured princess happened upon a frog in a pond.

The frog said to the princess, 'I was a handsome prince until an evil witch put a spell on me. One kiss from you and I will turn back into a prince and then we can marry, move into the castle with my mom and you can prepare my meals, clean my clothes, bear my children and forever feel happy doing so.'

That night, while the princess dined on frog legs, she laughed to herself and thought, 'I don't f***ing think so.'

A man who smelled like a distillery flopped on a subway seat next to a priest.

The man's tie was stained, his face was plastered with red lipstick, and a half-empty bottle of gin was sticking out of his torn coat pocket. He opened his newspaper and began reading.

After a few minutes the dishevelled guy turned to the priest and asked, 'Excuse me, Father, but what causes arthritis?'

'Mister, it's caused by loose living, being with cheap, wicked women, too much alcohol and a contempt for your fellow man.'

'Well, I'll be damned,' the drunk muttered, returning to his paper.

The priest, thinking about what he had said, nudged the man and apologised. 'Listen, I'm very sorry. I didn't mean to come on so strong. How long have you had arthritis?'

'Oh, *I* don't have it, Father. I was just reading here that the *Pope* does.

FOR SALE BY OWNER
Complete set of Encyclopaedia Britannica. 45 volumes.
Excellent condition.

**£1,000 or nearest offer. No longer needed. Got
married last weekend. Wife knows everything.**

A newly-wed farmer and his wife were visited by her
mother, who immediately demanded an inspection of the
place.

The farmer had genuinely tried to be nice to his new
mother-in-law, hoping that it could be a friendly, non-
antagonistic relationship. All to no avail though, as she
kept nagging them at every opportunity, demanding
changes, offering unwanted advice, and generally making
life unbearable for the farmer and his new bride.

While they were walking through the barn, during the
inspection, the farmer's mule suddenly reared up and
kicked the mother-in-law in the head, killing her instantly.

It was a shock to all, regardless of their feelings
towards her demanding ways...

At the funeral service a few days later, the farmer
stood near the casket and greeted folks as they walked
by.

The pastor noticed that whenever a woman would
whisper something to the farmer, he would nod his head
yes and say something.

Whenever a man walked by and whispered to the
farmer, however, he would shake his head no, and
mumble a reply.

Very curious about this bizarre behaviour, the pastor
later asked the farmer what that was all about.

The farmer replied, 'The women would say, "What a terrible tragedy" and I would nod my head and say, "Yes, it was." The men would then ask, "Can I borrow that mule?" and I would shake my head and say, "No can do, it's all booked up for a year."'

A man was taking his wife, who was pregnant with twins, to the hospital when his car went out of control and crashed.

Upon regaining consciousness, he saw his brother, a relentless, world-class practical joker, sitting at his bedside.

He asked his brother how his wife was and his brother replied, 'Don't worry, everybody is fine and you have a son and a daughter. But the hospital was in a real hurry to get the birth certificates filed and since both you and your wife were unconscious, I named them for you.'

The husband was thinking to himself, Oh no, what has he done now? and said with trepidation, 'Well what did you name them?'

The brother replied, 'I named the little girl Denise.'

The husband, relieved, said, 'That's a very pretty name! What did you come up with for my son?'

The brother replied, 'Denephew.'

The woman applying for a job in a Florida lemon grove seemed way too qualified for the job.

'Look, Miss,' said the foreman, 'have you any actual experience in picking lemons?'

'Well... as a matter of fact, yes!' she replied. 'I've been divorced three times.

Two buddies, Bob and Earl, were two of the biggest baseball fans in America. Their entire adult lives, Bob and Earl discussed baseball history in the winter, and they pored over every box score during the season.

They went to six games a year. They even agreed that whoever died first would try to come back and tell the other if there was baseball in heaven.

One summer night, Bob passed away in his sleep after watching the Yankee victory earlier in the evening. He died happy.

A few nights later, his buddy Earl awoke to the sound of Bob's voice from the beyond.

'Bob is that you?' Earl asked.

'Of course it's me,' Bob replied.

'This is unbelievable!' Earl exclaimed. 'So tell me, is there baseball in heaven?'

'Well, I have some good news and some bad news for you. Which do you want to hear first?'

'Tell me the good news first.'

'Well, the good news is that yes there is baseball in heaven, Earl.'

'Oh, that is wonderful! So what could possibly be the bad news?'

'You're pitching tomorrow night.'

Two atoms were walking down the street one day, when they bumped into each other.

One of them loses an electron and says, 'Ah shite, I've just lost a feckin' electron.'

The other replies, 'Are you sure?'

'Yes,' says the other, 'I'm feckin' positive.'

A man who lived in a block of apartments thought it was raining and put his head out the window to check. As he did so, a glass eye fell into his hand.

He looked up to see where it came from, in time to see a young woman looking down.

'Is this yours?' he asked.

She said, 'Yes, could you bring it up?' and the man agreed.

On arrival she was profuse in her thanks and offered the man a drink.

As she was very attractive he agreed.

Shortly afterwards she said, 'I'm about to have dinner. There's plenty – would you like to join me?'

He readily accepted her offer and both of them enjoyed a lovely meal.

As the evening was drawing to a close the lady said, 'I've had a marvellous evening. Would you like to stay the night?'

The man hesitated, then said, 'Do you act like this with every man you meet?'

'No,' she replied, 'only those who catch my eye.'

A cab driver reaches the Pearly Gates and announces his presence to St Peter, who looks him up in his Big Book.

Upon reading the entry for the cabbie, St Peter invites him to grab a silk robe and a golden staff and to proceed into Heaven.

A preacher is next in line behind the cabby and has been watching these proceedings with interest.

He announces himself to St Peter. Upon scanning the preacher's entry in the Big Book, St Peter furrows his brow and says, 'Okay, we'll let you in, now take that cloth robe and wooden staff.'

The preacher is astonished and replies, 'But I am a man of the cloth. You gave that cab driver a gold staff and a silk robe. Surely I rate higher than a cabbie.'

St Peter responded matter-of-factly, 'Here we are interested in results. When *you* preached, people slept. When the *cabbie* drove, people prayed.'

A man was complaining to a friend:

'I had it all – money, a beautiful house, a big car, the love of a beautiful woman ... then ... pow! ... just like that it was all gone!'

'Why, what happened?' asked the friend.

'Awww, my wife found out.'

Nancy and Bernie, two elderly widows in a Florida adult community, are curious about the latest arrival in their building . . . a quiet, nice-looking gentleman who keeps to himself.

Bernie says, 'Nancy, you know I'm shy. Why don't you go over to him at the pool and find out a little about him. He looks so lonely.'

Nancy agrees, and later that day at the pool, she walks up to him and says, 'Excuse me, mister, I hope I'm not prying, but my friend and I were wondering why you looked so lonely.'

'Of course I'm lonely,' he says, 'I've spent the past twenty years in prison.'

'You're kidding! What for?'

'For killing my third wife. I strangled her.'

'What happened to your second wife?'

'I shot her.'

'And, if I may ask, your first wife?'

'We had a fight and she fell off a building,'

'Oh my,' says Nancy. Then, turning to her friend on the other side of the pool, she yells, 'Yoo hoo, Bernie. He's single.'

Two music lovers were being held hostage and both were going to be shot.

One of them was a country music lover and the other enjoyed all kinds of music.

Before they were shot they were asked for one last request before they died.

The country music lover said, 'I would like to listen to "Achy Breaky Heart" fifty times in a row.'

The other music lover says, 'Please, shoot me first.'

In a small town there was a mine that completely collapsed.

'Hey bartender,' said the engineer, 'I'll have a beer and pour another one for my friend down at the end there.'

The bartender responded, 'I'm sorry sir but that guy's a commie and we don't serve his kind around here.'

'Well, you'd better because if it weren't for that guy, I wouldn't be here. You remember that mine that caved in? Well I was in that mine and so was that guy. When the last of us were escaping, he held the roof of the mine up with his head! So get him a beer and if you don't believe me, look at the top of his head and you'll see that it's flat from holding the roof up.'

The barman sceptically served the commie his beer and then came back to talk to the engineer. 'I saw the flat spot on his head but I also couldn't help noticing the bruising under his chin. What is that all about?' he asked.

The engineer replied, 'Oh . . . that's where we put the jack.'

Ten-year-old Ian rushes home from school. He invades the fridge and is scooping out some cherry-vanilla ice cream when his mother enters the kitchen.

She says, 'Put that away, Ian. You can't have ice cream now. It's too close to suppertime. Now go outside and play.'

Ian whimpers and says, 'There's no one to play with.'

Trying to placate him, she says, 'OK, I'll play with you. What do you want to play?'

He says, 'I wanna play Mommie and Daddy.'

Trying not to register surprise, and to further appease him, she says, 'Fine, I'll play. What do I do?'

Ian says, 'You go up to the bedroom and lie down.'

Figuring that she can easily control the situation Mom goes upstairs.

Ian, feeling a bit cocky, swaggers down the hall and opens the utility closet. He dons his father's old fishing hat. As he starts up the stairs he notices a cigarette butt in the ashtray on the end table. He picks it up and slips it into the corner of his mouth. At the top of the stairs he moves to the bedroom doorway.

His mother raises her head and says, 'What do I do now?'

In a gruff manner, Ian says, 'Get down those stairs and get that kid some ice cream!'

A truck driver frequently travelled through a small town where there was a courthouse at the side of the road. Of course, there were always lawyers walking along the road.

The truck driver made it a practice to hit any pedestrian lawyers with his truck as he sped by.

One day, he spotted a priest walking along the road and stopped to give him a ride. A little further along, as he approached the town, he spotted a lawyer walking along the side of the road.

Automatically, he veered his truck towards the lawyer, but ... then he remembered his passenger. He swerved back to the centre, but he heard a whump and in the rear view mirror he spotted the lawyer rolling across the field.

He turned to the priest and said, 'Father, I'm sure that I missed that lawyer.'

And the priest replied, 'That's OK, my son. I got him with the door.'

What's the difference between government bonds and men?
Bonds mature.

What do an anniversary and a toilet have in common?
Men always miss them.

A pompous clergyman was seated next to an overbearing attorney on a flight to Wichita.

After the plane was airborne, the flight attendant came around for drinks orders.

The attorney asked for a whiskey and soda, which was brought and placed before him.

The attendant then asked the minister if he would also like a drink.

The minister replied in disgust, 'I'd rather be savagely attacked and taken prisoner by a brazen hussy than let liquor touch these lips.'

The attorney then handed his drink back to the attendant and told her with delight, 'Sorry, I didn't know there was a choice.'

An Englishman, an Irishman and a Scotsman were in a pub, talking about their sons.

'My son was born on St George's Day,' commented the Englishman. 'So we decided to call him George.'

'That's a real coincidence,' remarked the Scot. 'My son was born on St Andrew's Day, so we decided to call him Andrew.'

'My God that's amazing,' said the Irishman. 'Exactly the same thing happened with *my* son, Pancake.'

There once was a young woman who went to Confession.

Upon entering the confessional she said, 'Forgive me, Father, for I have sinned.'

The priest replied, 'Confess your sins and be forgiven.'

'Last night, my boyfriend made mad passionate love to me seven times.'

The priest thought long and hard and then said, 'Take seven lemons, squeeze them into a glass, and then drink the juice.'

'Will this cleanse me of my sins, Father?'

'No, but it will certainly wipe that smile off your face.'

In some foreign country a priest, a lawyer and an engineer are about to be guillotined.

The priest puts his head on the block, they pull the rope and nothing happens. He declares that he has been saved by divine intervention, so he is let go.

The lawyer is put on the block, and again the rope doesn't release the blade. He claims he can't be executed twice for the same crime and he is set free too.

They grab the engineer and shove his head into the guillotine. He looks up at the release mechanism and says, 'Wait a minute, I see your problem...'

An eighty-five-year-old man marries a lovely twenty-five-year-old woman.

Because her new husband is so old the woman decides that on their wedding night they should have separate suites.

She is concerned that the old fellow could over-exert himself. After the festivities she prepares herself for bed and for the knock on the door she is expecting.

Sure enough the knock comes and there is her groom ready for action.

They unite in conjugal union and all goes well, whereupon he takes his leave of her and she prepares to go to sleep for the night.

After a few minutes there's a knock on the door and there the old guy is again, ready for more action. Somewhat surprised, she consents to further coupling, which is again successful, after which the octogenarian bids her a fond goodnight and leaves.

She is certainly ready for slumber at this point and is close to sleep for the second time when there is another knock at the door and there he is again, fresh as a twenty-five-year-old and ready for more.

Once again they do the horizontal boogie. As they're lying in the afterglow the young bride says to him, 'I am really impressed that a guy your age has enough energy to go for it three times. I've been with guys less than half your age who were only good for one.'

The old guy looks puzzled and turns to her and says, 'Was I already here?'

Three dead bodies turn up at the mortuary, all with very big smiles on their faces.

The coroner calls the police to show them what's happened.

A Detective Inspector is sent and is taken straight to the first body.

'Englishman, sixty, died of heart failure whilst making love to his mistress. Hence the enormous smile, Inspector,' says the coroner.

The DI is taken to the second dead man.

'Scotsman, twenty-five, won a thousand pounds on the lottery, spent it all on whisky. Died of alcohol poisoning, hence the smile.'

Nothing unusual here, thinks the DI, and asks to be shown the last body.

'Ah,' says the coroner,' this is the most unusual one. Irishman, thirty, struck by lightning.'

'Why is he smiling then?' inquires the DI.

'Thought he was having his picture taken,' replies the coroner.

A guy is walking past a big wooden fence at the insane asylum and he hears all the residents inside chanting, 'Thirteen! Thirteen! Thirteen!'

Quite curious about this, he finds a hole in the fence, and looks in.

Someone inside pokes him in the eye.

Then everyone inside the asylum starts chanting, 'Fourteen! Fourteen! Fourteen!'

A rabbit dashes in front of a car.

The driver screeches to a stop and jumps out. Too late! The rabbit is dead. As the man stands there wondering what to do, a woman drives up and stops to see what's happening.

The man says, 'I've just killed a rabbit in the middle of the road! What should I do?'

The woman thinks for a moment and then says, 'I think I have just the thing.'

She rummages through her trunk and produces a little bottle. She pours the contents onto the rabbit.

Miraculously, the rabbit jumps up, shakes itself, looks around, then hops off. It goes a few feet, then turns and waves, goes a few more feet, then turns and waves again.

This odd behaviour continues until the rabbit is out of sight.

The man looks at the woman in amazement and says, 'Wow! What did you do?'

The lady responds, 'I gave it a hair revitalizer with a permanent wave.'

While out one morning in the park, a jogger found a brand new tennis ball, and seeing no one around it might belong to, he slipped it into the pocket of his shorts.

Later, on his way home, he stopped at the pedestrian crossing, waiting for the lights to change.

A blonde girl standing next to him eyed the large bulge in his shorts. 'What's that?' she asked, her eyes gleaming with lust.

'Tennis ball,' came the breathless reply.

'Oh,' said the blonde sympathetically, 'that must be painful! I had tennis elbow once.'

A brunette goes into a doctor's office.

Brunette: 'Doctor, I don't know what's wrong with me.'

Doctor: 'Well, tell me your symptoms.'

Brunette: 'Well, everything hurts. When I touch my nose it hurts (touching nose), when I touch my leg it hurts (touching leg), when I touch my arm it hurts (touching arm), it just hurts everywhere!'

Doctor (after looking at her for a second): 'Were you ever a blonde?'

Brunette: 'Why yes!'

Doctor: 'Your finger's broken.'

Patient to doctor, 'You've got to help me, some mornings I wake up and think I'm Donald Duck. Other mornings I think I'm Mickey Mouse.'

Doctor: 'Hmmmm, and how long have you been having these Disney spells?'

Four expectant fathers were in Minneapolis hospital waiting room, while their wives were in labour.

The nurse arrived and announced to the first man, 'Congratulations sir, 'you're the father of twins.'

'What a coincidence,' the man said with obvious pride.

'I work for the Minnesota Twins baseball team.'

The nurse returned in a little while and turned to the second man, 'You, sir, are the father of triplets.'

'Wow, that's really an incredible coincidence,' he answered. 'I work for the 3M Corporation. My buddies at work will never let me live this one down.'

An hour later, while the other two men were passing cigars around, the nurse came back. This time she turned to the third man, who had been quiet in the corner. She announced that his wife had just given birth to quadruplets.

Stunned, he could barely reply.

'Don't tell me! Another coincidence?' asked the nurse.

After finally regining his composure, he said, 'I don't believe it. I work for the Four Seasons Hotel.'

After hearing this, everybody's attention turned to the fourth guy, who had just fainted, flat out on the floor. The nurse rushed to his side and after some time, he slowly regained his consciousness.

When he was finally able to speak, you could hear him whispering the same phrase over and over again.

'I should have never taken that job at 7-Eleven...'

'I should have never taken that job at 7-Eleven...'

'I should have never taken that job at 7-Eleven...'

It seems a man, wanting to rob a downtown Bank of America, walked into the branch and wrote 'This iz a stikkup. Put all your muny in this bag.'

While standing in line, waiting to give his note to the teller, he began to worry that someone had seen him write the note and might call the police before he reached the teller window.

So he left the Bank of America and crossed the street to Wells Fargo. After waiting a few minutes in line, he handed his note to the Wells Fargo teller. She read it and, surmising from his spelling errors that he was not the brightest light in the harbour, told him that she could not accept his stick-up note because it was written on a Bank of America deposit slip and that he would either have to fill out a Wells Fargo deposit slip or go back to Bank of America.

Looking somewhat defeated, the man said OK and left.

The Wells Fargo teller then called the police, who arrested the man a few minutes later, as he was waiting in line back at Bank of America.

A missionary who had spent years showing a tribe of natives how to farm and build things to be self-sufficient gets word that he is to return home.

He realises that the one thing he never taught the natives was how to speak English, so he takes the chief and starts walking in the forest.

He points to a tree and says to the chief, 'This is a tree.'

The chief looks at the tree and grunts, 'Tree.'

The missionary is pleased with the response.

They walk a little further and the padre points to a rock and says, 'This is a rock.' Hearing this, the chief looks and grunts, 'Rock.'

The padre is getting really enthusiastic about the results when he hears a rustling in the bushes.

As he peeks over the top, he sees a couple in the midst of heavy romantic activity. The padre is really flustered and quickly responds, 'Riding a bike.'

The chief looks at the couple briefly, pulls out his blow gun and kills them.

The padre goes ballistic and yells at the chief that he has spent years teaching the tribe how to be civilised and kind to each other, so how could he just kill these people in cold blood that way?

The chief replied, 'That's my bike.'

There's this old priest who got sick of all the people in his parish who kept confessing to adultery. One Sunday, in the pulpit, he said, 'If I hear one more person confess to adultery, I'll quit!'

Well, everyone liked him, so they came up with a code word.

Someone who had committed adultery would say they had fallen. This seemed to satisfy the old priest and things went well, until the priest died at a ripe old age.

About a week after the new priest arrived, he visited the mayor of the town and seemed very concerned.

The priest said, 'You have to do something about the sidewalks in town. When people come into the confessional, they keep talking about having fallen.'

The mayor started to laugh, realising that no one had told the new priest about the code word. Before the mayor could explain, the priest shook an accusing finger at the mayor and said, 'I don't know what you're laughing about, your wife fell three times this week.'

A motorist was unknowingly caught in an automated speed trap that measured his speed using radar and photographed his car.

He later received in the mail a ticket for £50 and a photo of his car.

Instead of payment, he sent the police department a photograph of £50.

Several days later, he received a letter from the police that contained another picture ... of handcuffs.

'So I got home, and the phone was ringing. I picked it up, and said "Who's speaking please?" And a voice said "You are."'

'So I rang up my local swimming baths. I said "Is that the local swimming baths?"
    He said, "It depends where you're calling from."

'So I was in my car, and I was driving along, and my boss rang up, and he said, "You've been promoted." And I swerved. And then he rang up a second time and said, "You've been promoted again." And I swerved again. He rang up a third time and said "You're managing director. And I went into a tree. And a policeman came up and said, "What happened to you?" And I said, "I just careered off the road."

'So I was getting into my car, and this bloke says to me, "Can you give me a lift?" I said "Sure, you look great, the world's your oyster, go for it."'

'And the back of his anorak was leaping up and down, and people were chucking money to him.
    I said, "Do you earn a living doing that?"
    He said, "Yes, this is my *livelihood*."

'So I went down my local ice cream shop, and said "I want to buy an ice cream." He said, "Hundreds and thousands?" I said, "We'll start with one."

He said, "Knickerbocker glory?"

I said, "I do get a certain amount of freedom in these trousers, yes."

'So I went to the dentist. He said, "Say Aaah." I said, "Why?"

He said, "My dog's just died."

'Now, most dentists' chairs go up and down, don't they? The one I was in went back and forwards. I thought, "This is unusual." And the dentist said to me, "Mr Cooper, would you mind getting out of the filing cabinet."

'So I rang up a local building firm. I said, "I want a skip outside my house."

He said, "Go ahead, there's no one stopping you."'

Nelson Mandela is sitting at home watching the telly when he hears a knock at the door.

When he opens it, he is confronted by a little Chinese man clutching a clipboard and yelling: 'You sign! You sign!' Behind him is an enormous truck full of car exhausts.

Nelson is standing there in complete amazement when the Chinese man starts to yell louder, 'You sign! You sign!'

Nelson says to him, 'Look mate, you've obviously got the wrong bloke. Sod off,' and shuts the door in his face.

The next day he hears a knock at the door again. When he opens it, the little Chinese man is back, with a huge truck full of brake pads. He thrusts his clipboard under Nelson's nose, yelling, 'You sign! You sign!'

Mr Mandela is getting a bit hacked off by now, so he shoves the little Chinese man back, shouting, 'Look, sod off! You've got the wrong bloke! I don't want them!' then slams the door in his face again.

The following day Nelson is resting, and late in the afternoon, he hears a knock on the door again. Upon opening the door, the little Chinese man thrusts the same clipboard under his nose, shouting, 'You sign! You sign!'

Behind him are TWO large trucks full of car parts.

Nelson loses his temper completely, picks the little man up by his shirt front and yells at him, 'Look, I don't want these! Do you understand? You must have the wrong name! Who do you want to give these to?'

The little Chinese man looks at him a bit puzzled, consults his clipboard, and says:

'You not Nissan Maindealer?'

It's World Cup final day at Le Stade de France and a young man is very disappointed when he finds his cheap seat is at the very rear of the stand, with a poor view of the pitch.

A few seconds after kick-off, he notices there is an empty seat near the front, so he wanders up and casually sits down. After ten minutes, he turns to the old man next to him. 'What kind of idiot would book seats this good,' he says, 'and not bother to turn up?'

'Actually,' the old man says, 'the seat is mine. I reserved it for my wife but now she's deceased. We've been coming to the World Cup finals since 1962 – in fact this is the first time that I've ever been without her.'

'Oh, my goodness,' the young man says, 'I'm very sorry. But tell me, isn't there anyone else you could have given a seat to, a son or daughter, perhaps?'

'Oh, I couldn't do that,' the old man says. 'They're all at the funeral.'

One day, two old men were sitting on the front porch of their retirement home.

One man says to the other, 'Ya know, Bill, if you think about it, we are not that old. I mean, my memory is still very good.'

As the man said this, he knocked on the wood chair beside him. 'Actually, it's as sharp as ever.'

After a couple of minutes of silence, the first man started to talk again.

'So, is *anyone* going to get the door or do I have to do it?'

A local business was looking for office help. They put a sign in the window, stating, 'HELP WANTED. Must be able to type, must be good with a computer and must be bilingual. We are an Equal Opportunity Employer.'

A short time afterwards, a dog trotted up to the window, saw the sign and went inside. He looked at the receptionist and wagged his tail, then walked over to the sign, looked at it and whined.

Getting the idea, the receptionist got the office manager. The office manager looked at the dog and was surprised, to say the least.

However, the dog looked determined, so he led him into the office.

Inside, the dog jumped up on the chair and stared at the manager. The manager said, 'I can't hire you. The sign says you have to be able to type.'

The dog jumped down, went to the typewriter and proceeded to type out a perfect letter.

He took out the page and trotted over to the manager and gave it to him, then jumped back on the chair. The manager was stunned, but then told the dog that he would have to be good with a computer.

The dog jumped down again and went to the computer. The dog proceeded to enter and execute a perfect program that worked flawlessly the first time.

By this time the manager was totally dumbfounded!

He looked at the dog and said, 'I realise that you are a very intelligent dog and have some interesting abilities. However, I still can't give you the job.'

The dog jumped down and went to a copy of the sign and put his paw on the sentences that told about being an Equal Opportunity Employer. The manager said, 'Yes, but the sign also says that you have to be bilingual.'

The dog looked at the manager calmly and said 'Meow.'

A farmer named Muldoon lived alone in the Irish countryside with a pet dog he doted on.

The dog finally died and Muldoon went to the parish priest and said, 'Father, the dog is dead. Could you please say a Mass for the creature?'

Father Patrick replied, 'No, we cannot have services for an animal in the church, but there's a new denomination down the road – no telling what they believe, but maybe they'll do something for the animal.'

Muldoon said, 'I'll go right now. Do you think £50,000 is enough to donate for their services?'

Father Patrick asked, 'Why didn't you tell me the dog was Catholic?'

Sherlock Holmes and Watson were on a camping and hiking trip.

They had gone to bed and were lying there looking up at the sky.

Holmes said, 'Watson, look up. What do you see?'

'Well, I see thousands of stars.'

'And what does that *mean* to you?'

'Well, I suppose it means that of all the planets and suns and moons in the universe, we are truly the one most blessed with the reason to deduce theorems to make our way in this world of criminal enterprises and blind greed. It means that we are truly small in the eyes of God but struggle each day to be worthy of the senses and spirit we have been blessed with. And, I suppose, at the very least, in the meteorological sense, it means that it is most likely that we will have another nice day tomorrow. What does it mean to you, Holmes?'

'To me, Watson, it means someone has stolen our tent.'

A woman was thinking about finding a pet to help keep her company at home.

She decided she would like to find a beautiful parrot; it wouldn't be as much work as a dog, and it would be fun to hear it speak. She went to a pet shop and immediately spotted a large, beautiful parrot. She went to the owner of the store and asked how much it was. The owner said it was £50. Delighted that such a rare-looking, beautiful bird wasn't more expensive, she agreed to buy it. The owner looked at her and said, 'Look, I should tell you first that this bird used to live in a house of ill-repute. Sometimes it says pretty vulgar stuff.'

The woman thought about this, but decided she had to have the bird.

She said she would buy it anyway. The pet shop owner sold her the bird and she took it home. She hung the bird's cage up in her living room and waited for it to say something. The bird looked around the room, then at her, and said, 'New house, new madam.'

The woman was a bit shocked at the implication, but then thought, 'That's not so bad.' A couple of hours later, the woman's two teenage daughters returned from school. When they inspected the bird, it looked at them and said, 'New house, new madam, new ladies.'

The girls and the woman were a bit offended at first, but then began to laugh about the situation. A couple of hours later, the woman's husband came home from work. The bird looked at him and said, 'New house, new madam, new ladies; same old faces . . . Hi George!!!!'

Jack decided to go skiing with his buddy, Bob. They loaded up Jack's stationwagon and headed north. After driving for a few hours, they got caught in a terrible blizzard. They pulled into a nearby farmhouse and asked the attractive lady of the house if they could spend the night.

'I'm recently widowed,' she explained, 'and I'm afraid the neighbours will talk if I let you stay in my house.'

'Not to worry,' Jack said, 'we'll be happy to sleep in the barn.'

Nine months later, Jack got a letter from the widow's attorney. He called up his friend Bob and said, 'Bob, do you remember that good-looking widow at the farm we stayed at?'

'Yes, I do.'

'Did you happen to get up in the middle of the night, go up to the house and have sex with her?'

'Yes, I have to admit that I did.'

'Did you happen to use my name instead of telling her your name?'

Bob's face turns red and he said, 'Yeah, I'm afraid I did.'

'Well, thanks! She just died and left me everything!'

Two guys were sitting outside a medical clinic. One of them was crying, tears pouring down his face.

The other guy asked, 'Why are you crying?'

The first one replied, 'I came here for blood test.'

The second one asked, 'So? Why are you crying? Are you afraid?'

The first guy replied, 'No, it's not that. During the blood test they cut my finger.'

Hearing this, the second one started crying.

The first one was astonished and asked the other, 'Why are you crying?'

Then the second guy replied, 'I have come for a urine test.'

A man walks into a house of ill repute in Reno and says, 'I'll give $20,000 to any woman here who'll come into the desert with me and do it MY way.'

One of the ladies agrees, and off they go driving into the desert.

After about an hour she gets curious, and asks him, 'Just what is *your* way?'

'On credit.'

Before they invented drawing boards, what did they go back to?

Two nuns, Sister Marilyn and Sister Helen, are travelling through Europe in their car. They get to Transylvania and are stopped at a traffic light.

Suddenly, out of nowhere, a diminutive Dracula jumps onto the hood of the car and hisses through the windshield.

'Quick, quick!' shouts Sister Marilyn. 'What shall we do?'

'Turn the windshield wipers on. That will get rid of the abomination,' says Sister Helen.

Sister Marilyn switches them on, knocking the little Dracula about, but he clings on and continues hissing at the nuns. 'What shall I do now?' she shouts.

'Switch on the windshield washer. I filled it up with Holy Water in the Vatican,' says Sister Helen.

Sister Marilyn turns on the windshield washer. Dracula screams as the water burns his skin, but he clings on and continues hissing at the nuns.

'Now what?' shouts Sister Marilyn.

'Show him your cross,' says Sister Helen.

'Now you're talking,' says Sister Marilyn as she opens the window and shouts, 'Get down off the bonnet of this car RIGHT F****ing* NOW!'

A fellow decides to leave early from work and go drinking.

He stays until the bar closes at 2 am, at which time he is extremely drunk.

When he enters his house, he doesn't want to wake anyone, so he takes off his shoes and starts tiptoeing up the stairs. Halfway up the stairs, he falls over backwards and lands flat on his rear end. That wouldn't have been so bad, except that he had a couple of empty pint bottles in his back pockets, and they broke, and the broken glass carved up his buttocks terribly. But he was so drunk that he didn't know he was hurt.

A few minutes later, as he was undressing, he noticed blood, so he checked himself out in the mirror, and, sure enough, his behind was cut up something terrible. Well, he repaired the damage as best he could under the circumstances, and he went to bed.

The next morning, his head was hurting, and his rear was hurting, and he was hunkering under the covers trying to think up some good story, when his wife came into the bedroom.

'Well, you really tied one on last night,' she said. 'Where'd you go?'

'I worked late,' he said, 'and I stopped off for a couple of beers.'

'A couple of beers? That's a laugh,' she replied. 'You got plastered last night. Where the heck did you go?'

'What makes you so sure I got drunk last night, anyway?' he asked.

'Well,' she replied, 'my first big clue was when I got up this morning and found a bunch of Band-Aids stuck to the mirror.'

Her marriage into high society was an excuse for Lady Upstart to invite princes and diplomats to her candlelit suppers and to put on airs and graces above her station.

It all got up the butler's nose.

But it turned out that on one of these society occasions her stomach was suffering a little internal turbulence and during an unfortunate lull in the conversation she let forth an audible fart.

Without batting an eyelid she turned briskly on the butler and said, 'Jeeves, stop that.'

Jeeves was up to the mark, 'Certainly madam, which way did it go?'

Two Irishmen are walking along Kensington High Street when they see a sign. 'Suits £15, Shirts £5, Trousers £8.' One says to the other one, 'Look at that – we could buy a lot of that gear and when we get back to Ireland we could make a fortune. When we go into the shop don't say anything. Let me do all the talking 'cause if they hear our accent they might not serve us so I'll speak in my best English accent.'

They go in and he orders fifty suits at £750, one hundred shirts at £500 and fifty pairs of trousers at £400.

The owner of the shop says, 'You lads are Irish aren't you?'

The guy said 'Damn . . . Yes, how the hell did you know that?'

The owner says, 'This is a dry cleaners . . .'

One fine day in Ireland, a guy is out golfing and gets up to the sixteenth hole.

He tees up and cranks one. Unfortunately, it goes into the woods on the side of the fairway.

He goes looking for his ball and comes across this little guy with the golf ball lying right beside him.

'Goodness,' says the golfer, and proceeds to revive the poor little guy.

Upon awaking, the little guy says, 'Well, you caught me fair and square. I am leprechaun. I will grant you three wishes.'

The man says, 'I can't take anything from you, I'm just glad I didn't hurt you too badly,' and walks away. Watching the golfer depart, the leprechaun thinks to himself, 'Well, he was a nice enough guy, and he did catch me, so I have to do something for him. I'll give him the three things that I would want. I'll give him unlimited money, a great golf game and a great sex life.'

Well, a year goes by and the same golfer is out golfing on the same course at the sixteenth hole.

He gets up and hits one into the same woods and goes off looking for his ball.

When he finds the ball he sees the same little guy and asks how he is doing.

The leprechaun says, 'I'm fine, and might I ask how your golf game is?'

'It's great! I hit under par every time'

'I did that for you. And might I ask how your money is holding out?'

The golfer says, 'Well, now that you mention it, every time I put my hand in my pocket, I pull out a £100 note.'

'I did that for you too. And might I ask how your sex life is?'

The golfer looks at him a little shyly and says, 'Well, maybe once or twice a week.'

The leprechaun is floored and stammers, 'What?! Only once or twice a week?'

'Well, that's not too bad for a Catholic priest in a small parish.'

Three guys are about to be executed and they are asked what they wish to have for their last meal.

The Italian responds, 'Pepperoni pizza', which he is served, and then he is executed.

The Frenchmen requests a filet mignon, which he is served, and then he is executed.

The Irishman requests a plate of strawberries.

'STRAWBERRIES ????'

'Yes, strawberries.'

He is told, 'But they are out of season!'

'So . . . I'll wait . . .'

A man called Mick with a winking problem is applying for a position as a sales representative for a large firm.

The interviewer looks over his papers and says, 'This is phenomenal. You've graduated from the best schools, your recommendations are wonderful and your experience is unparalleled. Normally, we'd hire you without a second thought. However, a sales representative has a highly visible position, and we're afraid that your constant winking will scare off potential customers. I'm sorry . . . we can't hire you.'

'But wait,' Mick said. 'If I take two aspirin, I'll stop winking!'

'Really? Great! Show me!'

So Mick reaches into his jacket pocket and begins pulling out all sorts of condoms: red condoms, blue condoms, ribbed condoms, flavoured condoms; finally, at the bottom, he finds a packet of aspirin. He tears it open, swallows the pills, and stops winking.

'Well,' said the interviewer, 'that's all well and good, but this is a respectable company, and we will not have our employees womanising all over the country!'

'Womanising? What do you mean? I'm a happily married man!'

'Well then, how do you explain all these condoms?'

'Oh, that,' says Mick. 'Have you ever walked into a pharmacy, winking, and asked for aspirin?'

Two cannibals in the South American rainforest came across an aircraft which crashed into the mountainside.

Inside they found a clown, who looked rather chewy and chubby, so they decided to take him outside and see how he tasted. They decided to take an arm each. The first cannibal took a chunk out of his upper arm and the other started just below the elbow.

Suddenly the first cannibal stopped eating and said, 'Hold on a minute, do you taste something funny?'

A young man goes to a doctor for a physical examination.

When he gets into the room, the man strips for his exam.

He has a 'thing' the size of a little kid's finger.

A nurse standing in the room sees his little 'thing' and begins to laugh hysterically.

The young man gives her a stern look and says, 'You shouldn't laugh, it's been swollen like that for two weeks now!'

With the ever- increasing changes in the communications business these days, it's wise to remember how easily this wonderful technology can be misused, sometimes unintentionally, with serious consequences.

Consider the case of the Illinois man who left the snow-filled streets of Chicago for a vacation in Florida. His wife was on a business trip and was planning to meet him there the next day.

When he reached his hotel, he decided to send his wife a quick e-mail.

Unable to find the scrap of paper on which he had written her e-mail address, he did his best to type it in from memory.

Unfortunately, he missed one letter and his note was directed instead to an elderly preacher's wife, whose husband had passed away only the day before. When the grieving widow checked her e-mail, she took one look at the monitor, let out a piercing scream, and fell to the floor in a dead faint. At the sound, her family rushed into the room and saw this note on the screen:

DEAREST WIFE:
JUST GOT CHECKED IN. EVERYTHING PREPARED FOR YOUR ARRIVAL TOMORROW.
P.S. SURE IS HOT DOWN HERE

A senator walks into a restaurant and is seated at one of the finest tables.

A particularly voluptuous waitress comes to his table wearing a short skirt with legs that won't quit.

'What would you like, Senator?' she asks.

The senator looks at the menu and then scans her beautiful frame top to bottom, and answers, 'A quickie.'

The waitress stomps off in total disgust. After she regains her composure she returns and asks again, 'What would you like, Senator?'

Again he thoroughly checks her out and again answers, 'A quickie, please.' This time her anger takes over.

She reaches over and slaps him across the face with a resounding 'SMACK!' and storms away.

A Secret Service agent, sitting at the next table, leans over and whispers, 'Um, excuse me, Senator, but I think it's pronounced "QUICHE".'

Two blondes walked into a building.

You'd think one of them would have seen it!

Here's a story I did on *The 2FM Breakfast Show* last Christmas which led to a lot of requests for a copy of it. Just make sure the kids don't see it!

Does Santa exist?

There are approximately two billion children (persons under 18) in the world.

However, since Santa does not visit children of Muslim, Hindu, Jewish or Buddhist (except maybe in Japan) religions, this reduces the workload for Christmas night to 15 per cent of the total, or 378 million (according to the Population Reference Bureau). At an average (census) rate of 3.5 children per household, that comes to 108 million homes, presuming that there is at least one good child in each.

Santa has about 31 hours of Christmas to work with, thanks to the different time zones and the rotation of the earth, assuming he travels east to west (which seems logical). This works out to 967.7 visits per second. This is to say that for each Christian household with a good child, Santa has around 1/1000th of a second to park the sleigh, hop out, jump down the chimney, fill the stockings, distribute the remaining presents under the tree, eat whatever snacks have been left for him, get back up the chimney, jump into the sleigh and get on to the next house.

Assuming that each of these 108 million stops is evenly distributed around the earth (which, of course, we know to be false, but will accept for the purposes of our calculations), we are now talking about 0.78 miles per household; a total trip of 75.5 million miles, not counting bathroom stops or breaks. This means Santa's sleigh is moving at 650 miles per second . . . 3,000 times the speed of sound. For purposes of comparison, the fastest man-made vehicle, the *Ulysses* space probe, moves at a poky 27.4 miles per second, and a conventional reindeer can run (at best) at 15 miles per hour.

The payload of the sleigh adds another interesting element.

Assuming that each child gets nothing more than a medium-sized Lego set (two pounds), the sleigh is carrying over 500,000 tons, not counting Santa himself. On land, a conventional reindeer can pull no more than 300 pounds. Even granting that the 'flying' reindeer could pull ten times the normal amount, the job can't be done with eight or even nine of them – Santa would need 360,000 of them. This increases the payload, not counting the weight of the sleigh, another 54,000 tons, or roughly seven times the weight of the *Queen Elizabeth* (the ship, not the monarch).

Six hundred thousand tons travelling at 650 miles per second creates enormous air resistance – this would heat up the reindeer in the same fashion as a spacecraft re-entering the earth's atmosphere.

The lead pair of reindeer would absorb 14.3 quintillion joules of energy per second each.

In short, they would burst into flames almost instant-aneously, exposing the reindeer behind them and creating deafening sonic booms in their wake. The entire reindeer team would be vaporised within 4.26 thousandths of a second, or right about the time Santa reached the fifth house on his trip.

Not that it matters, however, since Santa, as a result of accelerating from a dead stop to 650 mps. in 0.001 seconds, would be subjected to acceleration forces of 17,500 gs. A 250-pound Santa (which seems ludicrously slim) would be pinned to the back of the sleigh by 4,315,001 pounds of force, instantly crushing his bones and organs and reducing him to a quivering blob of pink goo.

Therefore, if Santa did exist, he's dead now . . . Merry Christmas!

A newly elected governor was giving a large party to celebrate his inauguration.

All the local gentry were invited, as were some of the governor's old military buddies.

During the party, a sweet young thing thought she might have some fun with a stiff-looking military man dressed in navy blues. So she walked over and asked him when was the last time he had had sex.

'1956,' was his immediate reply.

'No wonder you look so uptight!' she exclaimed. 'Honey, you need to get out more.'

'I'm not sure I understand you,' he answered, glancing at his watch. 'It's only 2014 now.'

Walking into the bar, Paul said to the bartender, 'Pour me a stiff one, Eddie. I just had another fight with the wife.'

'Oh yeah,' said Eddie. 'And how did this one end?'

'When it was over,' Paul replied, ' She came to me on her hands and knees.'

'Really? Wow! Well, that's certainly a change! What did she say?'

Paul (sheepishly): 'She said, 'Paul, come out from under the bed, you gutless weasel!'

This blonde babe really wanted to go ice fishing.

She'd seen many books on the subject, and finally, after getting all the necessary tools together, she made for the nearest frozen lake. After positioning her comfy footstool, she started to make a circular cut in the ice. Suddenly, from the sky a voice boomed, 'THERE ARE NO FISH UNDER THE ICE!'

Startled, the blonde moved further down the ice, poured a Thermos of cappuccino, and began to cut yet another hole. Again, from the heavens, the voice bellowed, 'THERE ARE NO FISH UNDER THE ICE!'

The blonde, now quite worried, moved way down to the opposite end of the ice, set up her stool, and tried again to cut her hole. The voice came once more, even louder, 'THERE ARE NO FISH UNDER THE ICE!'

She stopped, looked skyward, and said, 'Is that you, Lord?'

The voice replied:

'NO, THIS IS THE ICE RINK MANAGER!'

Dave works hard at the factory and spends most evenings bowling or playing basketball at the gym. His wife thinks he is pushing himself too hard, so for his birthday she takes him to a local strip club.

The doorman at the club greets them and says, 'Hey, Dave, how ya doin'?'

His wife is puzzled and asks if he's been to this club before. 'Oh no,' says Dave. 'He's on my bowling team.'

When they are seated, a waitress asks Dave if he'd like his usual Budweiser.

His wife is becoming uncomfortable and says, 'You must come here a lot for that woman to know you drink Budweiser.'

'No, honey, she's in the ladies bowling league. We share lanes with them.'

Just then, a stripper comes over to their table and throws her arms around Dave.

'Hi, Davey,' she says, 'want your usual table dance?'

Dave's wife, now furious, grabs her purse and storms out of the club.

Dave follows and spots her getting into a cab. Before she can slam the door, he jumps in beside her and she starts screaming at him.

The cabby turns his head and says, 'Looks like you picked up a right wild one tonight, Dave.'

Two elderly ladies meet at the launderette after not having seen one another for some time. After inquiring about each other's health, one asked how the other's husband was doing.

'Oh! Ted died last week. He went out to the garden to dig up a cabbage for dinner, had a massive heart attack and dropped down dead right there in the middle of the vegetable patch!'

'Oh dear! I'm very sorry,' replied her friend 'What did you do?'

'Opened a can of peas instead.'

A duck walks into a bar and says, 'Got any bread?'

The barman says, 'No,' and the duck says, 'Got any bread?'

And the barman again says, 'No!'

'Got any bread?' asks the duck again.

'I said, NO!'

'Got any bread?'

'For crying out loud. "N" "O" spells NO and I mean NO!!'

'Got any bread?'

'NO NO NO NO NO NO NO NO NO NO NO NO!!!'

'Got any bread?'

'Look, if you ask me one more f***ing time if I've got any bread, I'm going to nail your f***ing beak to the f***ing bar!!'

'Got any nails?'

'No!'

'Got any bread?'

Did you hear about the gay magician?

He disappeared with a poof!

A girl and a boy were at the back of the cinema, kissing passionately.

When they come up for air, the boy says, 'I really love kissing you, but would you mind not passing me your chewing gum.'

The girl replies, 'It's not chewing gum, I've got bronchitis.'

An angry wife met her husband at the door.

There was alcohol on his breath and lipstick on his collar. 'I assume,' she snarled, 'that there is a very good reason for you to come waltzing in here at six o'clock in the morning?'

'There is,' he replied. 'Breakfast.'

What is the one thing that all men who visit singles bars have in common?

They're married.

What do you call a woman who knows where her husband is every night?

A widow.

What's got ninety balls and makes women sweat?

Bingo.

What makes men chase women they have no intention of marrying?

The same urge that makes dogs chase cars they have no intention of driving.

Fresh out of business school, the young man answered a wanted ad for an accountant.

Now he was being interviewed by a very nervous man who ran a small business that he had started himself.

'I need someone with an accounting degree,' the man said. 'But mainly, I'm looking for someone to do my worrying for me.'

'Excuse me?' the accountant said.

'I worry about a lot of things,' the man said. 'But I don't want to have to worry about money. Your job will be to take all the money worries off my back.'

'I see,' the accountant said. 'And how much does the job pay?'

'I'll start you at eighty thousand.'

'Eighty thousand dollars!' the accountant exclaimed. 'How can such a small business afford that kind of money?'

'That,' the owner said, 'is your first worry.'

A rather attractive woman goes up to the bar in a quiet rural pub.

She gestures alluringly to the barman, who comes over immediately.

When he arrives, she seductively signals that he should bring his face close to hers.

When he does so, she begins to gently caress his beard, which is full and bushy.

'Are you the landlord?' she asks, softly stroking his face with both hands.

'Actually, no,' he replies.

'Can you get him for me – I need to speak to him?' she asks, running her hands up beyond his beard and into his hair.

'I'm afraid I can't,' breathes the barman, clearly aroused. 'Is there anything I can do?'

'Yes there is. I need you to give him a message,' she continues huskily, popping a couple of fingers into his mouth and allowing him to suck them gently.

'Tell him that there is no toilet paper in the ladies room.'

How many men does it take to change a roll of toilet paper?

We don't know; it has never happened.

A pensioner couple went back on holiday to the place where they first met. So they're sitting in the pub and he says to her, 'Remember our first time together about forty years ago. We went round the corner to the gasworks. You leaned against the fence and I made passionate love to you.'

'Yes,' she says, 'I remember it well.'

'Well,' he says, 'how about taking a stroll round there and I'll give you one for old times' sake.'

'Sounds like a lovely idea,' she answers.

So there's a chap sitting at the next table listening to all this, having a chuckle to himself, and he thinks, 'I've got to see this, two pensioners making out against the gasworks fence.'

So he follows them. They get to the gasworks, they lean against the fence, start kissing and before long they're getting down to business, and he is going hell for leather like an eighteen-year-old.

The other chap is peeping round the corner at this time thinking, My God, he can't half go for a pensioner.

After about forty minutes the old couple finish and get their clothes back on. The guy watching thinks, that was amazing, he was going like a train. I've got to ask him what his secret is.

As the couple pass the chap says, 'That was something else, you must have been going non-stop for about forty minutes there. How do you manage it? Is there some sort of secret?'

'No, there's no secret,' the man says, 'but forty years ago that fence wasn't electrified.'

124

Next time you're having a bad day . . . think of this story from the *California Examiner:*

Fire authorities in California found a corpse in a burnt-out section of forest while assessing the damage done by a forest fire. The deceased male was dressed in a full wetsuit, complete with a dive tank, flippers and face mask. A post-mortem examination revealed that the person died not from burns but from massive internal injuries.

Dental records provided a positive identification.

Investigators then set about determining how a fully clad diver ended up in the middle of a forest fire. It was revealed that, on the day of the fire, the person went for a diving trip off the coast, some twenty miles away from the forest. The firefighters, seeking to control the fire as quickly as possible, called in a fleet of helicopters with very large buckets. The buckets were dropped into the ocean for rapid filling, then flown to the forest fire and emptied.

You guessed it.

One minute our diver was making like Flipper in the Pacific, the next he was doing a breaststroke in a fire bucket 300 feet in the air.

Apparently, he extinguished exactly 5'10" of the fire. Some days it just doesn't pay to get out of bed!

The following is taken from a Florida newspaper

A man was working on his motorcycle on his patio and his wife was in the house in the kitchen. The man was racing the engine on the motorcycle and somehow, the motorcycle slipped into gear. The man, still holding the handlebars, was dragged through a glass patio door and, along with the motorcycle, dumped onto the floor inside the house.

The wife, hearing the crash, ran into the dining room, and found her husband lying on the floor, cut and bleeding, the motorcycle lying next to him and the patio door shattered.

The wife ran to the phone and summoned an ambulance.

Because they lived on a fairly large hill, the wife went down the several fights of long steps to the street to direct the paramedics to her husband.

After the ambulance arrived and transported the husband to the hospital, the wife uprighted the motorcycle and pushed it outside. Seeing that gas had spilled on the floor, the wife obtained some paper towels, blotted up the gasoline, and threw the towels in the toilet.

The husband was treated at the hospital and was released to come home.

After arriving home, he looked at the shattered patio door and the damage done to his motorcycle. He became despondent, went into the bathroom, sat on the toilet and smoked a cigarette. After finishing the cigarette, he flipped it between his legs into the toilet bowl while still seated. The wife, who was in the kitchen, heard a loud explosion and her husband screaming. She ran into the bathroom and found her husband lying on the floor. His trousers had been blown away and he was suffering burns on the buttocks, the back of his legs and his groin.

The wife again ran to the phone and called for an ambulance.

The same ambulance crew was dispatched and the wife met them at the street. The paramedics loaded the husband on the stretcher and began carrying him to the street. While they were going down the stairs to the street accompanied by the wife, one of the paramedics asked the wife how the husband had burned himself. When she told them, the paramedics started laughing so hard, one of them tipped the stretcher and dumped the husband out.

He fell down the remaining steps and broke his two arms!

Now *that's* what you call a *bad* day!

A priest is walking down the street one day when he notices a very small boy trying to press a doorbell on a house across the street. However, the boy is very small and the doorbell is too high for him to reach.

After watching the boy's efforts for some time, the priest moves closer to the boy's position.

He steps smartly across the street, walks up behind the little fellow and, placing his hand kindly on the child's shoulder, leans over and gives the doorbell a solid ring.

Crouching down to the child's level, the priest smiles benevolently and asks, 'And now what, my little man?'

The boy replies, 'Now Father . . . we run!'

Little Lizzy came home from school and was heard by her mother reciting her homework:

'Two plus two, the son of a bitch is four; four plus four, the son of a bitch is eight; eight plus eight, the"son of a bitch . . . '

'Lizzy!' shouted her mother. 'You watch your language! You're not allowed to use swear words like "son of a bitch".'

'But, Mom,' replied Lizzy, 'that's what the teacher taught us, and she said to recite it out loud till we learned it.'

Next day Lizzy's mother went to school with her daughter and marched right into the classroom to complain.

'Oh, good heavens!' said the teacher. 'That's not what I taught them. They're supposed to say, "Two plus two, the sum of which is four".'

'That wife of mine is a liar,' said an angry husband to a sympathetic pal seated next to him in the bar.

'How do you know?' the friend asked.

'Well, she didn't come home last night and when I asked her where she'd been, she said she had spent the night with her sister, Shirley.'

'So?'

'So she's a liar. I spent the night with Shirley.'

As a senior citizen called Harold was driving down the motorway, his car phone rang.

Answering, he heard his wife's voice urgently warning him, 'Harold, I just heard on the news that there's a car going the wrong way on the M50. Please be careful!'

'Boy,' said Harold, 'It's not just one car. There are *hundreds* of them!'